W9-BON-990

SPEED TOYS FOR BOYS

A SCOOTER CONTEST.

SPEED TOYS FOR BOYS

(and for Girls, Too)

Armand J. LaBerge

Instructor in Manual Arts, Bryant Junior High School,
Minneapolis, Minn. Assistant Supervisor of Play-
grounds, Boys' and Men's Activities during the
summer months, Minneapolis Park Board.

LINDEN PUBLISHING, INC.
Fresno, California

Speed Toys for Boys

by

Armand J. LaBerge

135798642

Cover art by James Goold

Printed in the U.S.A.

ISBN: 978-1-933502-18-2

The plans presented in this book were developed nearly 80 years ago and may not meet the strict safety standards of today. Please use common sense when constructing and using these toys. The publishers accept no legal responsibility for any consequences, which may arise, from the advice, information, and instructions in this book.

Library of Congress Cataloging-in-Publication Data

LaBerge, Armand J.
  Speed toys for boys (and for girls, too) / Armand J. LaBerge.
    p. cm.
  Originally published: Milwaukee, Bruce Pub. Co., 1928.
  ISBN 978-1-933502-18-2 (pbk. : alk. paper)
  1. Woodwork (Manual training)--Juvenile literature. 2. Scooters--Design and contruction--Juvenile literature. I. Title.
  TT157.L184 2008
  684'.08--dc22

                                                                    2007051747

Linden Publishing, Inc.
2006 S. Mary
Fresno, CA 93721
www.lindenpub.com
800-345-4447

PREFACE

THE purpose of this book is to suggest to boys, and to their teachers, a variety of worth-while recreational projects, and to furnish complete instructions and plans for such projects. The author has definitely kept in mind the boys' welfare and interest, and has chosen only such projects as have a place in the world of boys' interests, and the world in which boys spend their leisure time.

The materials required for the greater number of the projects presented are well adapted to the general school shops. Some of the projects are original; others are the result of adaptations made in the writer's classes. All of the projects are being made by boys in the writer's classes in Bryant Junior High School, Minneapolis, Minn., and the boys thoroughly enjoy making them.

The present trend in our great democracy is toward fewer working hours. This naturally means more leisure time. It is a generally accepted fact that the activities of boys and young people during their leisure time play a most important part in character building and in the formation of habits. It has been proved that evil associations, which lead to the downfall of boys, are formed most often during their leisure time. Manual-arts activities, through the making of boy projects at school and at home, contribute much toward the boy's valuable use of his leisure time. Every boy has some desire to create or build, or to express himself in his activities. Is it not true then, that if his inventive mind is given a chance to express itself through the work of his hands in the construction of some activity project in which he is interested, nothing but good habits and many happy, educational, leisure hours will be the result?

Boys entering a "pushmobile contest" in Minneapolis spent from four to six weeks before the contest preparing, designing, and building their cars. During a recent contest 2,500 boys were busy enjoying this fine leisure-time activity. A few of the pushmobiles were built during the school year in manual-arts shops of the city schools, but the majority of the cars were built in the boys' own shops or in their back yards. This is a most excellent example of the "carry over" effect of the many activities of the manual-arts shops of the schools.

The pushmobile handcraft activity is but one of the many handwork features for boys. In a scooter contest sponsored by the recreational department of the Minneapolis park board, 400 scooters were of the homemade type, made by boys at home or in the school shops. Sailboats and kites, too, are projects that thousands of boys construct each year.

It is the hope of the writer that this book may encourage such boy activities by suggestion, by stimulation of interest, and by practical instruction on the making of many worth-while projects.

The author acknowledges indebtedness to J. E. Painter, supervisor of manual training, Minneapolis, Minn., for much inspiration and many helpful suggestions; to Karl B. Raymond, director of recreation of the Minneapolis park board, and H. A. Johnson, assistant director of recreation for their splendid cooperation and for the use of pushmobile photographs, and scooter and pushmobile programs; and to the Minneapolis *Tribune* for the use of photographs of "pushmobile contests."

ALPHABETICAL LIST OF PROJECTS

TABLE OF CONTENTS

SPEED TOYS FOR BOYS

CHAPTER I
MATERIALS, TOOLS, AND PROCESSES

WOOD

THERE is a great variety in the qualities and uses of various kinds of wood. The following table will serve as a guide in selecting wood suitable for a given project:

Birch. Hard; strong; tough; heavy; easy to work; takes very good finish. Uses: Wheels; bolsters; axles; dowel rods; scooter-sleds; hobby cars, or any parts requiring hardwood.

Hickory. Straight; coarse; heavy; hard; very flexible and very strong. Uses: Ideal for toboggan runners; scootersleds; handles for tools; wheels, etc.

Oak. Strong; hard; flexible; heavy; splits easily; hard to nail; takes very good finish. Uses: Furniture; hobby cars; scooters; coaster wagons, or any parts requiring hardwood.

Ash. Straight; strong; light brown; works fairly well. Uses: Wheels; cabinetmaking; coaster wagons; axles; bolsters; toboggan runners, etc.

Butternut. Soft; very light; close, and straight grain; nails well; easy to work. Uses: Novelty boxes; carts; furniture, etc.; a good wood for pushmobile parts requiring light wood.

White Pine. Soft; light; close, and straight grain; easy to nail; easy to work. Uses: Boxes; carts; toys; pushmobile framework; toboggan runners, etc.

Basswood. Light; white; soft; close grained; durable; works easily. Uses: Toys; novelty boxes; carts; wood carving.

Tulip (Yellow Poplar). Soft; light; close grained; works very easily; a very good substitute for hardwood. Uses: Toymaking; wood carving; furniture, etc., almost any parts of boy projects.

SHEET METAL

The metals commonly used in the home or school shops are black iron, galvanized iron, and tin plate.

Black Iron is a soft-steel sheet which takes a very good paint and enamel finish. It is the best kind of metal to cover such projects as the kiddomobiles and pushmobiles.

Tin Plate consists of the same kind of soft metal coated with tin.

Galvanized Iron is also a soft-steel sheet with a coating of zinc. It does not take a paint or enamel finish very well unless it is given a special treatment. (See "Preparing Metal Surfaces," p. 16.)

The common size of sheets of galvanized and black iron is 30 by 96 in. This can be purchased from any sheet-metal shop or iron store. The wide-awake boy can always find enough discarded sheets or pieces of metal without going to the expense of buying new metal. The old metal can oftentimes be cleaned and sanded and made to look like new.

BAND IRON

Band iron is wrought iron manufactured in standard widths and thicknesses ranging from $\frac{3}{8}$ to 12 in. wide, and in almost any thickness from $\frac{1}{16}$ in. up. It is a very desirable metal to use where strength and flexibility are required. Band or bar iron can be twisted and hammered cold better than any other iron. It is considered the best kind of iron to use for welding. Band iron for home or school shop usually can be obtained from an iron store, a local blacksmith shop, or a hardware store. It is usually sold by the pound. The wide-awake boy can probably discover in his own back yard discarded pieces of band iron that he can use very successfully for braces or parts on some of the projects.

DRILLING IN IRON

Drilling in iron requires a little more exertion than boring in wood, but with a drill well sharpened, the drilling should be a simple matter and easily done. Before doing any drilling, the centers of all the holes should be located and marked. This is done with a center punch. The center-punch hole or mark will keep the drill point at the desired spot when starting the drill. When drilling in wrought iron (band iron), oil should be used on the point of the drill to prevent overheating.

The drilling can be done vertically or horizontally in a vise, depending on the drill holder used. The common brace used in boring wood can also be used with good results in drilling thin iron, such as $\frac{1}{16}$ to $\frac{3}{8}$ in. thickness. The hand and breast drills are very handy and efficient tools commonly used in drilling iron, when the post or power drills are not available. The lathe boring device illustrated in Plate 1 can be used in drilling iron with excellent results.

If two pieces of iron are to be fastened together with rivets, the holes for the rivets should be the size of the diameter of the

rivets used. If the iron parts are to be joined with bolts, drill the holes the size of the threaded portion of the bolt.

WOODEN WHEELS

Coping or Turning Saw. Flat wooden wheels may be easily cut with the coping or turning saw. With a pair of dividers set to the desired radius, describe a circle on the stock to be used. Make the circle line deep in the wood so it can be seen plainly. With a coping saw properly adjusted, cut to the line carefully. The coping saw should be held in a horizontal position as shown in Figure 1.

FIG. 1. THE COPING SAW SHOULD BE HELD
IN A HORIZONTAL POSITION.

When sawing with the coping saw it is best to use short fast strokes, and to apply very light pressure on the blade of the saw. The blade should be held at a right angle to the flat surface of the wheel at all times. If the sawing is done very carefully, the wheels should be neat and true. For heavier stock the turning saw may be used.

The wheels can be made more attractive by carving a groove with a gouge, ¾ or 1 in. from the rim of the wheel. A little patience and care is all that is necessary to accomplish this. Trim, and finish the wheels with a wood file and sandpaper.

tools free-hand, requires more skill than the average boy can command. It is suggested that some mechanical device or jig, such as those illustrated in Plate 1 and Figure 2, be employed. If a lathe is used to turn the wheels, a boring device can be easily attached to the lathe. (See Pl. 1 and Fig. 3.)

FIG. 3. BORING DEVICE.

Bushings. Pieces of iron pipe may be used as bushings for wooden wheels. Great care should be taken in boring a hole at the exact center of each wheel. (See "Boring Devices," Pl. 1 and Figs. 2 and 3.) The size of the hole should be equal to the outside diameter of the bushing or a trifle smaller.

Make a slit or groove on the outside of the bushing by sawing halfway through the thickness of the bushing with a hack saw. In like manner, using a coping saw through the hole of the wheel, make a slit or cut about ⅜ in. deep. Force the bushing into the hole of the wheel with a mallet. See that the cut in the bushing and the one in the wheel are in line with each other so that a steel key can be forced into the slits or grooves. A piece of a broken hack-saw blade makes an excellent key for this purpose. (See Plates 11 and 33.) Pieces of threaded iron pipe also make very good bushings.

FIG. 2. JIG FOR USE IN BORING.

Band Saw. Among the power machines suitable for this purpose are the band saw and the jig saw. If the band saw is used, the blade should not exceed ⅜ in. in width. Mark out the circle as above and saw carefully to the line. Trim to a nice finish with a wood file and sandpaper.

Boring in Wheels. The usual tools employed for this purpose are the brace and bit, but to bore a perfectly true hole with these

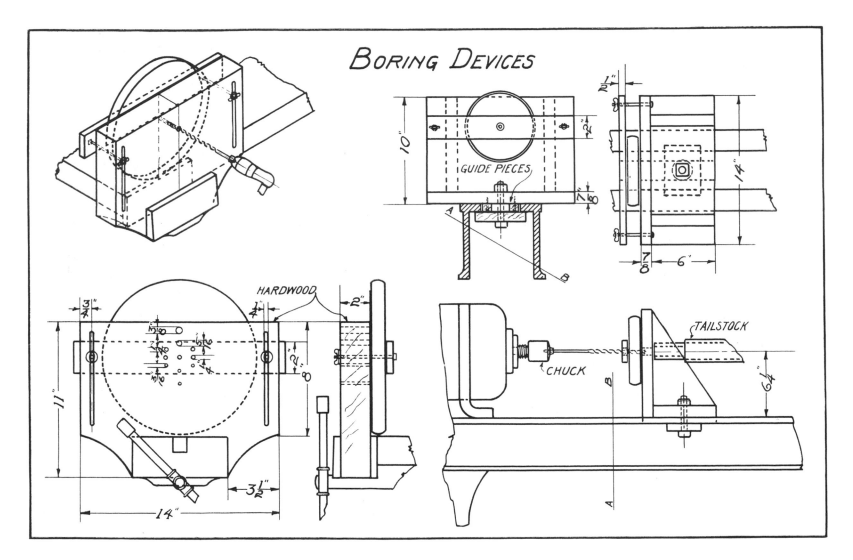

BORING DEVICES

PLATE 1.

DOUBLE-DISC WHEELS

Wheels of the double-disc type usually can be obtained from a local hardware store. Double-disc wheels of all sizes with axles suitable for hobby cars, coaster wagons, pushmobiles, etc.; casters and tea-wagon wheels for scooters, and steering irons for push-mobiles can be obtained from several manufacturers throughout the country.

TOOLS

The manual-arts instructors are often asked by boys and parents to recommend a list of tools for the home shop. Good tools make ideal birthday or Christmas gifts for boys.

It should be remembered that only good tools should be purchased. Cheap tools usually prove a very expensive investment in the long run and they never give satisfactory results.

It is recommended that a small number of tools of good quality be purchased at first. By adding new tools now and then when the funds are available, one can soon have a complete equipment that is sure to last for many years. A suggested list of tools is given below:

1 Jack Plane, 14 in.	1 Knife (Jack or Sloyd)
1 Try-Square, 6 in.	3 Chisels, 1 in., ½ in., and ¼ in.
1 Rule	1 Carpenters' Square
1 Crosscut Saw, 20 in., 10 point	1 Oilstone
1 Ripsaw, 22 in., 8 point	1 Brace and Set of Bits
1 Claw Hammer	1 Countersink
1 Marking Gauge	3 Twist Drills for Metal, $\frac{3}{16}$ in.
1 Screw Driver	3 Twist Drills for Metal, ¼ in.
1 Half-Round Wood File, No. 10	3 Twist Drills for Metal, $\frac{3}{8}$ in.
1 Coping Saw, 1 doz. blades	2 Gouges, 1 in., and ¾ in.
1 Nail Set	1 Pair Pliers
1 Pair Dividers	1 Pair Tinners' Snips
1 Spokeshave	1 Hack Saw
	1 Center Punch

THE FINISHING AND COLORING OF PROJECTS

A great deal of thought should be given to the finishing of projects illustrated in this book. The boy should consider the finish of this problem of as much importance as the making of it. Even though the greatest care may have been taken in the construction of a project, the very best piece of work can be spoiled by a hurried or poorly applied finish. It is not the intention of the writer to go into detail about wood finishing, but merely to give a few suggestions on how projects in this book may be treated.

Preparing Wood Surfaces. A good finish cannot be obtained on a rough surface. It is necessary therefore that every part of the project be thoroughly sanded. Use No. ½ and No. 00 sandpaper to get the surfaces smooth. Sand with the grain of the wood and dust off carefully.

Paint Finish. A very lasting and desirable finish may be obtained by using a simple gloss outside paint. Paint may be used on both wood and metal with good results. There are many good brands of common house paint on the market that can be obtained in different colors in small-size cans. The following colors may be purchased: yellow, red, blue and white. Any color can be produced by combining the three primary colors—yellow, red, and blue. (See "Color Chart," Pl. 2.) Often the alert boy can find odd lots of old house paint around the home which he can prepare instead of buying new paint.

After the surface has been prepared, apply a thin coat of white paint as a priming coat on the project to be finished. This coat should be rather thin and still not "run" when applied to vertical surfaces. After the priming coat is dry, fill nail holes and small defects in the wood with putty or hard wax. Sand with No. 00 sandpaper when perfectly dry. The second coat is given more than the usual amount of linseed oil to produce a gloss finish. Oil in paint produces a gloss finish while turpentine causes a dull or flat finish. If a third coat is needed, allow the second coat to dry thoroughly before sanding with No. 00 sandpaper, and apply a final gloss finish.

The surface to be finished should be prepared carefully. When the surface is perfectly smooth give the project a thin coat of white shellac. When this is dry, sand lightly with No. 00 sandpaper. Apply a coat of white paint, or other good undercoat for

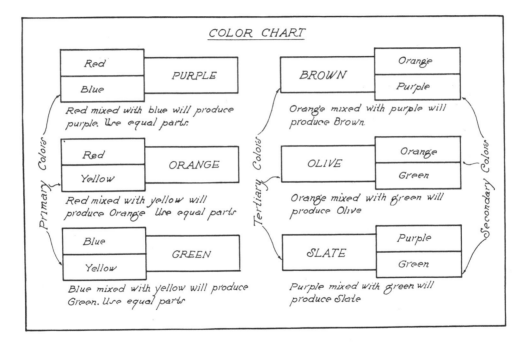

PLATE 2.

Enamels. Although enamels are more expensive than most finishes, they are by far the best and most desirable for the greater part of the projects listed in this book. They can be purchased prepared ready for use in all colors in small-size cans. The glossy finish of enamel is very attractive and is sure to appeal to every boy and girl.

enamel. This, of course, when dry, should be sanded with No. 00 sandpaper. One day or more should be allowed for this coat to dry thoroughly before sanding. Dust off the project carefully and apply a coat or two of the desired shade of enamel for the final finish. If two coats of enamel are given, the first coat, when thoroughly dry, must be sanded with No. 00 sandpaper before the

[Page 14]

second coat is applied. If the project is finished in more than one color, make sure that one color is dry before applying another color.

Tempera and Kalsomine Finishes. Tempera and kalsomine colors are known as show-card colors. They come under the heading of Water Colors. Tempera may be obtained in small jars in different colors ready for use. (See "Color Chart," Pl. 2.) Excellent results may be obtained on both wood and metal. Before applying the tempera, make sure that every part of the project has been thoroughly sanded. Apply a thin coat of tempera of the desired color to all parts of the project. If two colors are used, wait until one color is dry before applying another color next to it. When dry, sand *very lightly* with No. 4-0 sandpaper. Next, apply one coat of thin shellac and sand *this* very lightly with No. 4-0 sandpaper when dry. Apply a coat of good varnish as a final finish.

Kalsomine colors are sold in powder form. They are the cheapest of water-color finishes. Kalsomine powders are mixed with water and a small amount of glue before they are ready for use. One coat of the desired color of kalsomine may be applied to a project and finished according to the directions given for tempera.

Water Stains. Water stains are cheap; they are transparent, and penetrate the wood quite deep. They can be made of any coloring matter that dissolves in water. They may be purchased in powder form to be mixed, or in liquid form ready for use. They give better satisfaction on hardwood than on softwood.

Water stains raise the grain of the wood and are harder to apply than other stain finishes. Because they raise the grain, it is well to give the wood a special treatment before using water stains. Sponge the surface to be finished, with warm water, to raise the grain, and when dry, sand *very lightly* with No. 00 sandpaper. The object of this treatment is to provide a surface, the grain of which has already been raised. If the sanding is not done *very*

lightly, the raised grain will be cut away and the proper effect or the treatment will be lost.

Apply the stain hot with a brush or sponge. When the stain is dry, apply a thin coat of white shellac. When the shellac is dry, sand with No. 00 sandpaper. One or two coats of good varnish may be applied for the final finish. This may be rubbed down with pumice stone and water.

Oil Stains. Oil stains usually give better results than other stains. They may be purchased ready for use in any color or quantity, or they may be prepared by mixing colors in linseed oil or turpentine. The pigments commonly used for oil stains are burnt sienna, burnt umber, drop black, aniline dyes, chrome yellow, and Van Dyke brown. Different colors may be obtained by mixing or combining the above pigments. Oil stains do not raise the grain of the wood like water stains, but they can be used with excellent results on both softwood and hardwood.

Apply oil stains with a brush or cloth. Allow the stain to penetrate the wood for a short time and then wipe off with a cloth. When the stain is dry, apply one coat of thin white shellac as a filler. When dry, sand this with No. 00 sandpaper. One or two coats of spar varnish may be applied for the final finish. This may be rubbed down with pumice stone and water.

Lacquer. A very suitable finish, quite popular at present, is the new brushing lacquer. This finish can be used to good advantage on most of the projects in this book, especially on the smaller ones. Brushing lacquer may be obtained on the market in a great variety of colors and shades ready for use. It is suggested that the manufacturer's directions be closely followed when applying lacquer. The treatment suggested here is for new surfaces of wood or metal. (See "Preparing Metal Surfaces," p. 16.) The surface should be sanded smooth and all nail holes and defective places filled with water putty.

First, give the project a thin coat of shellac, and sand with No. 4-0 sandpaper when dry. Lacquer should be applied with a good quality fitch-hair brush or a camel's hair brush. Apply, or *flow on*, lacquer with a brush and do not brush over the same place more than once. Lacquer cannot be brushed back and forth like varnish or paint, and therefore must be *flowed on* very quickly.

Two or three coats are usually enough when applied over surfaces that have been treated with shellac. The last coat should be allowed to dry several hours before being sanded lightly with a No. 4-0 wet sandpaper. The sanding should be done in one direction only. Finally, the surface may be polished with rotten-stone and oil. If a dull effect is desired, the final sanding and rubbing may be omitted.

Preparing Metal Surfaces. Make sure that the metal surface to be finished is perfectly smooth. This can be done by sanding the metal with No. 00 sandpaper. All band-iron corners and sharp edges should be filed smooth so as to be free from any possible cutting edges.

Wash the surface and all metal parts with benzine or gasoline. When this is dry, the finish may be applied. If galvanized iron is used, the surface should be given a special treatment before paint and enamel are applied. Very good results may be obtained by applying vinegar to the galvanized surface to be finished. Allow the vinegar to become perfectly dry before applying the paint or enamel. For further information about painting on gal-

A RACER CONTEST.

vanized iron see "A Handbook on Japanning" by W. N. Brown, published by The D. Van Nostrand Co., New York City.

Metal Finishing. It is suggested that a simple gloss paint or a simple auto-enamel finish be applied to projects made of sheet metal. If a better finish is desired, consult a book on automobile finishing. Black iron may be either painted or enameled.

If a simple paint finish is desired, apply one thin coat of white paint or flat undercoating as a metal primer. Two days should be allowed for this to dry; then sand with No. 00 sandpaper. Apply another thin coat of white paint. When this coat is thoroughly dry, it should be rubbed smooth with No. 00 pumice stone and water. A felt pad, or a blackboard eraser, may be used for rubbing. Wash off all metal parts with water and allow the surface to become perfectly dry before applying the finish. One or two coats of paint of the desired color may be used as a finish. If two finishing coats are given, rub with pumice stone and water before applying the final coat. The directions for applying gloss paint vary with different kinds of paint. and it is well to follow directions given on the container.

A finer finish may be obtained by using automobile enamel for the finishing coats instead of paint. Although automobile enamel is more expensive than ordinary house paint, it is by far the best type of finish for metal. There are many good automobile enamels on the market that can be purchased ready for use in any quantity or color desired.

CHAPTER II
CARTS AND HOBBY CARS

HANDY CART

THE Handy Cart illustrated in Plate 3 is a simple and very interesting project. The little folks between the ages of 2 and 6 greatly appreciate a toy of this type.

Any softwood such as pine, butternut, basswood, or cypress may be used. It is best to make the wheels and bolster A of hardwood. A coping saw or turning saw may be used for cutting the wheels. Follow directions in Chapter I for making wheels.

Bill of Material. Finished dimensions.
2 pc. $\frac{3}{8}$ x $3\frac{1}{8}$ x $12\frac{1}{2}$ Sides of Box (C)
2 pc. $\frac{3}{8}$ x $3\frac{1}{8}$ x $6\frac{3}{4}$ Ends of Box (C)
1 pc. $\frac{3}{8}$ x $7\frac{1}{2}$ x $12\frac{1}{2}$ Bottom
1 pc. $\frac{3}{4}$ x $2\frac{1}{2}$ x 8 Bolster (A) (Hardwood)
1 pc. $\frac{3}{4}$ x $1\frac{3}{4}$ x 7 Block (B)
1 pc. $\frac{3}{4}$ x $\frac{7}{8}$ x 38 Handle (E)
1 pc. $\frac{3}{8}$ x $4\frac{7}{8}$ Dowel (F)
2 Wheels, $\frac{5}{8}$ in. thick, $5\frac{1}{2}$ in. diam. (D)

Assembling. Use glue and 1-in. brads in assembling the box C. The box is attached to bolster A with two 1-in. No. 8 f.h. screws. The handle is fastened to the box of the cart with a $\frac{3}{16}$ by 2-in. stove bolt, and to part A with a $1\frac{1}{2}$-in. No. 8 f.h. screw. A dowel, $\frac{3}{8}$ by $4\frac{7}{8}$ in., is used for the crosspiece of the handle. This is held in place by a brad nailed through the handle and dowel. Fasten the wheels to the ends of bolster A with 2-in. No. 12 r.h. screws.

Finishing. A suggested color scheme is given in the drawing. A simple gloss paint or lacquer, or a stain finish is suggested for this project. (See section on "Finishing and Coloring of Projects" in Chap. I.)

Handy Cart

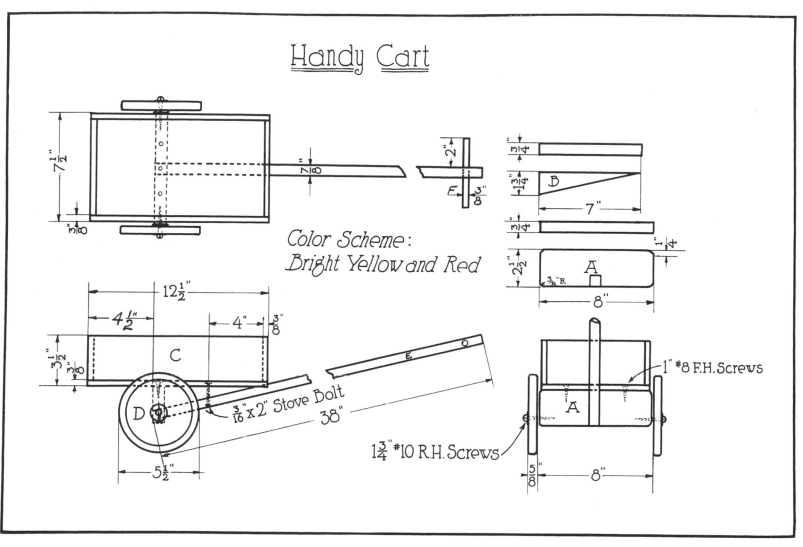

Color Scheme:
Bright Yellow and Red

$7\frac{1}{2}$"

$\frac{3}{8}$"

$\frac{7}{8}$"

2"

E

$\frac{3}{8}$"

$\frac{3}{4}$"

$\frac{3}{4}$"

$1\frac{3}{4}$"

B

7"

$\frac{3}{4}$"

$2\frac{1}{2}$"

$\frac{1}{4}$"

A

$\frac{3}{8}$"R

8"

$12\frac{1}{2}$"

$4\frac{1}{2}$"

4"

$\frac{3}{8}$"

C

$3\frac{1}{2}$"

$\frac{3}{8}$"

D

$\frac{3}{16}$" x 2" Stove Bolt

38"

E

$5\frac{1}{2}$"

1" #8 F.H. Screws

A

$1\frac{3}{4}$" #10 R.H. Screws

$\frac{5}{8}$"

8"

PLATE 3

[Page 19]

PONY AND CART

The Pony and Cart is always a popular toy with youngsters between the ages of 3 and 7. The pony head has a strong appeal to boys and girls of that age.

Bill of Material. Finished dimensions.
1 pc. ⅜ x 3½ x 6¼   One End of Box (D)
1 pc. ⅜ x 3⅛ x 6¼   One End of Box (D)
2 pc. ⅜ x 3 x 11   Sides of (D)
1 pc. ⅜ x 7 x 11   Bottom of (D)
1 pc. ¾ x 2¼ x 7½   Bolster (A) (Hardwood)
1 pc. ¾ x 1¼ x 3   Block (B) (Softwood)
1 pc. ¾ x ⅞ x 38   Handle (F) (Hardwood)
1 pc. ¾ x 8 x 12   Head (C) (Softwood or Hardwood)
1 pc. ⅞ in. diam. x 7 Dowel (G)
2 Wheels, ⅝ in. thick, 5½ in. diam. (Hardwood)

Box. The box part can be made first. Any softwood such as pine, butternut, or basswood may be used. Follow the drawings for shaping the ends and sides.

Pony Head. The pony head may be made from softwood or hardwood. If softwood is used, a close-grained wood like poplar is recommended.

On a piece of drawing paper, or heavy wrapping paper 8 by 12 in., lay out 1-in. squares. Follow the outline of the pony head in Plate 2. Notice where the curved line crosses each square and locate the same points on your chart. Connect these points with a line free-hand. When the pattern is drawn, cut to line carefully. Lay the pattern on the wood to be used and trace around it. With a coping saw, cut to this line and finish with a wood file and sandpaper.

Wheels. The wheels should be made of hardwood and they can best be turned on a lathe. If a lathe is not available, a neat

wheel may be made by using a coping saw or a turning saw. (See section on "Wooden Wheels" in Chap. I.)

Assembling. All parts of the cart should be sanded thoroughly before assembling. Use glue and 1-in. brads in assembling the box D. The box is attached to bolster A with 1-in. No. 8 f.h. screws. The handle is fastened to the box of the cart with a ³⁄₁₆ by 2-in. stove bolt, and to part A with a 1½-in. No. 8 f.h.

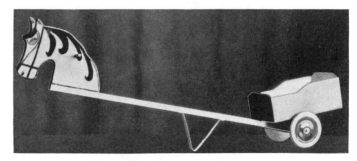

FIG. 4. PONY AND CART

screw. The pony head is fastened to one end of the handle with two 1½-in. No. 9 f.h. screws. A dowel, ½ by 6 in., is used for the crosspiece of the handle. Fasten the wheels to the ends of bolster A with 2-in. No. 12 r.h. screws. Washers should be used between the screw head and the wheel, also between the wheel and the cart.

Finishing. A suggested color scheme is given in the drawing. Stain, lacquer, or a simple gloss paint may be used on this project.

PONY AND CART

Color Scheme
A- Yellow   E- Red & Yellow
B- Yellow   C- Yellow & Black
D- Red

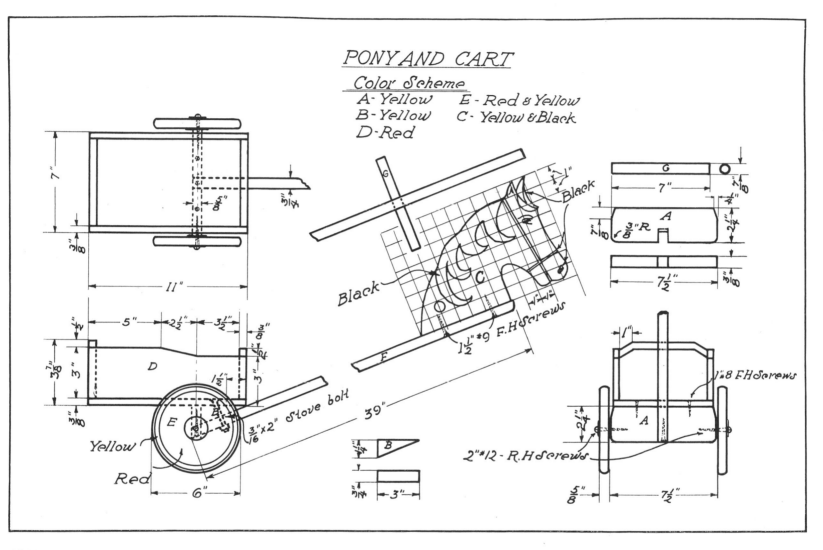

PLATE 4.

[Page 21]

A simple toy which is new and very fascinating to the youngster between the ages of 4 and 8 is the Tiger and Chariot illustrated in Plate 5. It may be called "The Hobby Tiger and Chariot." It will last a long time if made of hardwood. However, any softwood such as poplar, pine, or butternut may be used.

Bill of Material. Finished dimensions.

1 pc. $5/8$ x 7 x 10 Base (A)
1 pc. $7/8$ x $7/8$ x $9\frac{1}{4}$ Axle (B)
1 pc. $5/8$ x $3/4$ x 36 Tongue (C)
1 pc. $3/4$ x 8 x 10 Tiger (E)
1 pc. $3/8$ x 5 Dowel (F)
1 pc. $5\frac{1}{8}$ x 22 Black Iron No. 26 Gauge (G)
2 Wheels, $5/8$ in. thick, 5 in. diam. (D)

Base. Make the baseboard first. Round off the back and front ends as shown in the drawing. Cut to the line with a coping saw, and finish with a spokeshave, wood file, and sandpaper.

Tiger. It is best to make a pattern of the tiger on paper first. On a piece of drawing paper, or wrapping paper 8 by 10 in., lay out 1-in. squares as indicated in Plate 5. Notice where the outline crosses each square and locate the same points on your chart. Connect these points with a line. Trace this outline of the tiger on the stock to be used. Cut to the line with a coping saw, and finish with a wood file and sandpaper.

Wheels. The wheels can best be turned on a wood-turning lathe. If a lathe is not available, a neat wheel may be made with a coping saw. (See section on "Wooden Wheels" in Chap. I.)

TIGER AND CHARIOT

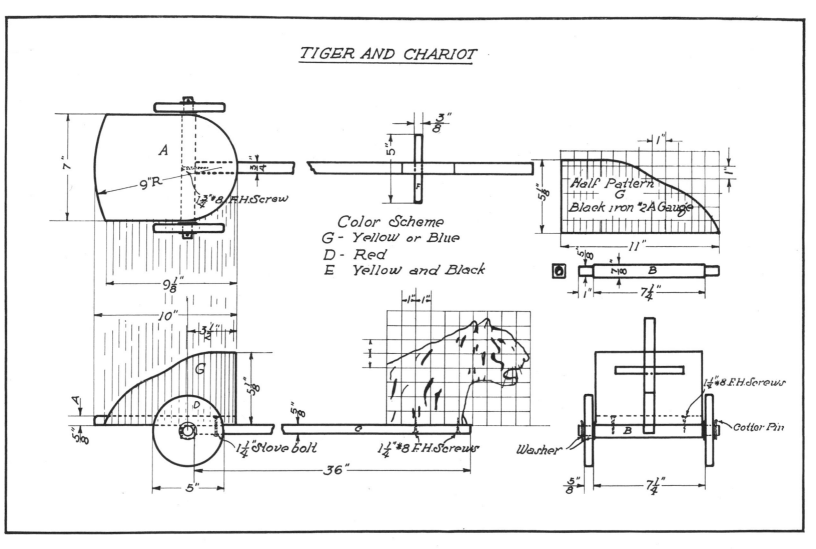

Color Scheme
G - Yellow or Blue
D - Red
E   Yellow and Black

PLATE 5.

[Page 23]

The Doll Cart illustrated in Plate 6 is greatly appreciated by little girls who enjoy playing with dolls. It makes a novelty carriage for dolly, and affords endless pleasure to its owner. It is best to make all wooden parts of the cart of hardwood. However, poplar, basswood, or pine may be substituted.

Bill of Material. Finished dimensions.

1 pc. $\frac{5}{8}$ x 8 x 10 Seat (A)
1 pc. $\frac{3}{4}$ x $2\frac{1}{2}$ x 9 Bolster (B)
1 pc. $\frac{3}{4}$ x $1\frac{1}{2}$ x $5\frac{3}{4}$ Triangle Block (D)
1 pc. $\frac{5}{8}$ x $1\frac{1}{2}$ x 37 Tongue (C)
1 pc. $1\frac{1}{16}$ x $\frac{1}{2}$ x $12\frac{1}{4}$ Leg (E) (Band Iron)
1 pc. $\frac{3}{8}$ in. diam. x $3\frac{1}{2}$ Dowel (G)
1 pc. $5\frac{5}{8}$ x 25 Black Iron No. 24 or 28 Gauge (F)
2 Wheels, $\frac{5}{8}$ in. thick, $6\frac{1}{2}$ in. diam. (H)

Seat. Make the seat first. Round off the back as shown in the drawing. Cut to the line with a coping saw and finish with a spokeshave, wood file, and sandpaper.

Body. The body F of the cart may be made of black iron No. 24 or 28 gauge. If the No. 28 gauge iron is used, the top edge of F should be turned. This can be done with a pair of pliers or on a turning machine. If the No. 24 gauge or heavy iron is used, file the top edge very smooth.

Wheels. The wheels can best be turned on a wood-turning lathe. If a lathe is not available, a neat wheel may be made by using a coping saw. (See section on "Wooden Wheels" in Chap. I.)

Assembling. Sandpaper all parts thoroughly before assembling. The seat A is fastened to bolster B with $1\frac{1}{4}$-in. No. 8 f.h. screws 7 in. from the front. Fasten the tongue C and the brace D to the seat with a $\frac{3}{16}$ by 2-in. stove bolt at point X. Fasten the lower end of the tongue to bolster B with a $1\frac{3}{4}$-in. No. 9 f.h. screw. The metal body F is attached to the seat A next. Nail the metal to the edge of A with $\frac{1}{2}$-in. escutcheon pins or box nails.

The wheels are fastened to the ends of bolster B, $\frac{3}{4}$ in. from the bottom, with 2-in. No. 12 r.h. screws. Use washers between the heads of the screws and the wheels, also between the wheels and the bolster. A piece of band iron, $\frac{1}{16}$ by $\frac{1}{2}$ by $12\frac{1}{4}$ in., is used

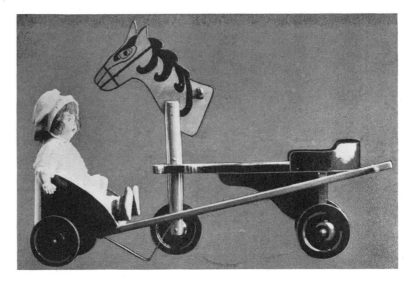

FIG. 5. DOLL CART AND HOBBY CAR.

for the tongue leg E. Bend the iron to the proper shape and fasten it to the tongue C with $\frac{3}{4}$-in. No. 7 r.h. screws.

Finishing. Tempera, gloss paint, enamel, or lacquer may be used to finish the doll cart. A suggested color scheme is given in the drawing. (See section on "Finishing and Coloring Projects" in Chap. I.)

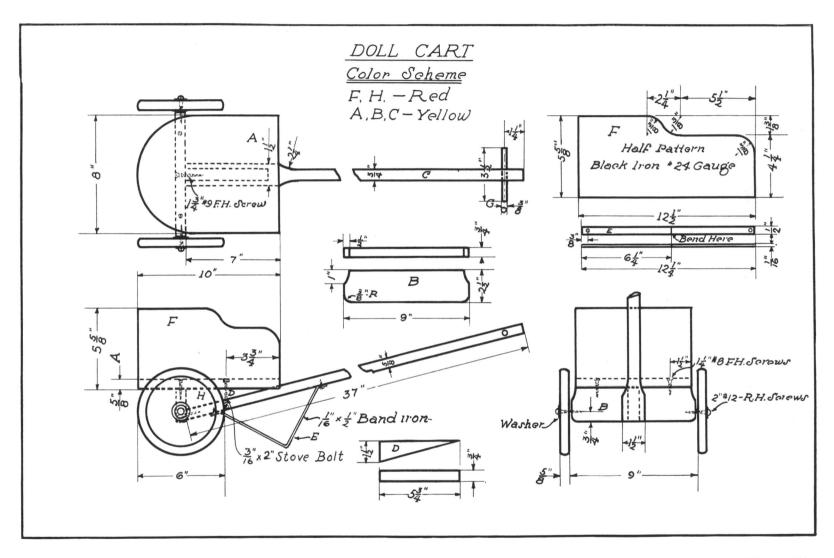

DOLL CART

Color Scheme

F, H, — Red

A, B, C — Yellow

PLATE 6.

[Page 25]

WHEELBARROW

The wheelbarrow illustrated in Plate 7 is rather simple in construction and affords a great deal of pleasure to the little folks.

Bill of Material. Finished dimensions.
2 pc. ⅝ x 7¼ x 18   Sides (B) (Softwood)
1 pc. ⅝ x 5¼ x 10   Front (D) (Softwood)
1 pc. ⅝ x 10   x 18   Bottom (A) (Softwood)
2 pc. ¾ x 1   x 33½ Handles (C) (Hardwood)
2 pc. ¾ x 1   x 2   Blocks (F)
2 pc. ⅛ x   ⅞ x 15   Legs (G) (Band Iron)
1 Bolt, ¼ x 3½ (Carriage Bolt)
1 Wheel, ¾ in. thick, 6 in. diam. (E) (Hardwood)

Body. The box part can be made of softwood. Make the sides B first and taper these pieces to 5¼ in. at one end as shown in the drawing. Round off the rear top corners, using a 2¼-in. radius. Follow the given dimensions for the front and bottom.

Handles. Make the handles C of hardwood (oak or birch). Round off one end of the handles as shown in Plate 7 for a distance of 6 in. This can be done with a spokeshave, wood file, and sandpaper.

Wheels. Make the wheel E of oak or birch ¾ in. thick and 6 in. in diameter. The wheel may be turned on a lathe or cut with a coping saw. (See section on "Wooden Wheels" in Chap. I, and Pl. 7.)

Legs. The two legs G are made of two pieces of band iron ⅛ by ⅞ by 15 in. Drill two holes at each end of the pieces G and bend them to the shape suggested in the drawing. The band iron may be held in a vise while the bending is being done.

Assembling. Use glue and 2-in. brads to assemble the box. The box is fastened to the handles C with 1¼-in. No. 9 f.h. screws. Make two blocks F and nail them on the inside of the handles at the front. Attach the wheel to the front of the handles C with a ¼ by 3½-in. carriage bolt. Use washers between the blocks F and the wheels. The two band-iron legs are fastened to the handles C with ¾-in. No. 8 r.h. screws at the points shown in the drawing.

Finishing. A paint, lacquer, or an oil stain may be used for finishing this project. (See section on "Finishing and Coloring of Projects" in Chap. I.) A suggested color scheme is given in Plate 7.

WHEEL BARROW

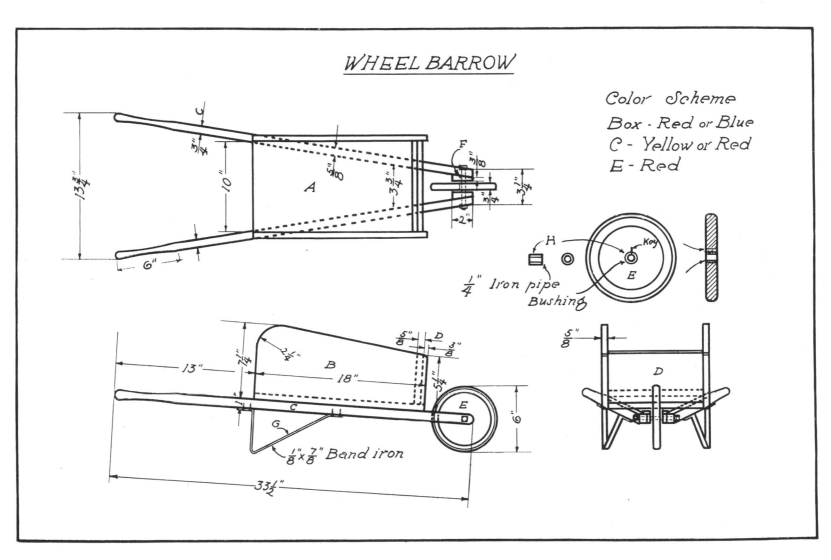

Color Scheme
Box - Red or Blue
C - Yellow or Red
E - Red

¼" Iron pipe Bushing

⅛" x ⅞" Band iron

PLATE 7.
[Page 27]

The Ice Cart shown in Plate 8 is a very handy and useful cart to have around any home. It may be used as an ice cart, a grocery wagon, or a play cart.

Bill of Material. Finished dimensions.

2 pc.	⅝ x 6 x 22	Sides of Box (A)
2 pc.	⅝ x 6 x 15	Ends of Box (A)
1 pc.	⅝ x 16¼ x 22	Bottom of (A)
2 pc.	½ x 1⅛ x 23	Sides of Frame (F)
2 pc.	½ x 1⅛ x 17	Ends of Frame (F)
1 pc.	1¼ x 4½ x 17¼	Bolster (B)
1 pc.	1¼ x 3 x 12½	Block (C)
1 pc.	⅞ x 1¾ x 38	Tongue (D)
1 pc.	⅛ x ⅞ x 19	Leg (F) (Band Iron)
1 pc.	⅜ in. diam. x 4	Dowel (E)
2 Wheels, about 10 in. diam. (Coaster-Wagon Wheels)		
1 Axle, ½ in. diam. Length to suit wheels (Steel Rod)		

Box. The box A may be made first. Any softwood such as pine, butternut, or basswood may be used.

Bolster. Shape the bolster B as indicated in Plate 8. A softwood may be used for B. With a ½-in. gouge, cut a groove into the bottom of B for an axle. Bore two holes, each 1 in. in diameter, through bolster B at points indicated in Plate 8.

Tongue. Make the tongue D of oak or birch, or any other suitable hardwood. A piece of dowel, ⅜ by 4 in., is used for the crosspiece.

Leg. The leg E is made of a piece of band iron. With a steel drill bore a $\frac{3}{16}$-in. hole at each end of E. Bend the iron as shown in Plate 8.

Wheels. Coaster-wagon wheels or any other available wheels may be used on this cart. The diameter of the axle will depend on the kind of wheels used. Drill a small hole at each end of the axle for cotter keys. Also, drill a $\frac{3}{16}$-in. hole 4½ in. from each end of the axle.

Assembling. The box A is assembled with 2-in. brads. Nail the frame F to the top of the box. The box is fastened to bolster B with 1½-in. No. 9 f.h. screws 7 in. from the back. Fasten the tongue D and brace C to the box of the cart with a ¼ by 3-in. carriage bolt, 5½ in. from the front of the cart. The lower end of the tongue D is attached to bolster B with a 2-in. No. 9 f.h. screw. Fasten the axle to bolster B with $\frac{3}{16}$ by 2-in. stove bolts. Use washers between the wheels and the bolster B, also between the wheels and the cotter keys. The band-iron leg E is attached to the tongue with a 1-in. No. 8 f.h. screw and a $\frac{3}{16}$ by 1-in. stove bolt.

Finishing. Use an outside paint to finish this project. (See section on "Finishing and Coloring of Projects" in Chap. I.) Any color combination to suit the individual's taste may be used.

ICE CART

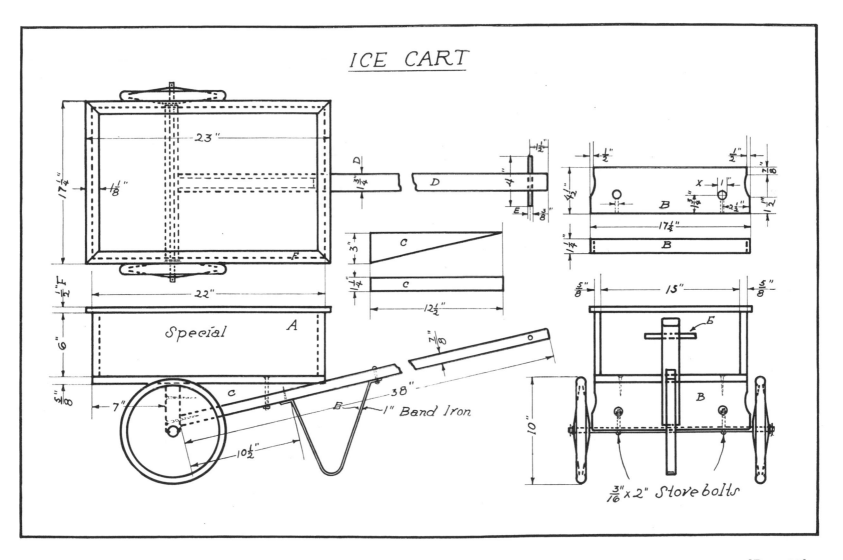

PLATE 8.

[Page 29]

The Hobby Car needs no introduction. It is always a very popular toy with little folks between the ages of 3 and 8. The pony head connected with this car is an added attraction and makes the car more popular than ever. A hardwood should be used in making this project. Birch or oak are very desirable. Poplar is the best of the softwoods for the purpose.

Bill of Material. Finished dimensions.

1 pc. 7/8 x 9 x 23   Seat (C)
1 pc. 3/4 x 6½ x 11   Brace (D)
1 pc. 7/8 x 8 x 7¾   Bolster (E)
1 pc. 3/4 x 14 x 12   Pony Head (A)
1 pc. 2¾ x 24½ Black Iron No. 28 Gauge, Back (J)
1 pc. 2 in. diam. x 7½ Steering Post (F)
1 pc. 2 in. diam. x 7   Steering Post (G)
1 pc. 1 in. diam. x 8   Handle (H)
1 pc. 7/8 in. diam. x 4½ Dowel Rod (I)
3 Wheels, 7/8 in. thick, 6 in. diam. (B)

Seat. It is well to make a pattern of the seat C on paper first. This pattern may be drawn on heavy wrapping paper or drawing paper. Then trace the pattern on the stock to be used. Cut to the line with a coping saw or a turning saw. Finish smooth with a spokeshave, wood file, and sandpaper. Bore a hole 7/8 in. in diameter through the front end, 2 in. from the end.

Bolster E and Brace D. Square these pieces carefully. Follow the directions and details given in Plate 9. Lay out the curved lines and cut to these lines with a coping saw. Finish the edges with a spokeshave, wood file, and sandpaper.

Wheels. The wheels for this car should be turned on a lathe. If a turning lathe is not available, neat wheels may be cut with a coping saw. A nice wheel with a pipe bushing is illustrated in Plate 11. (See section on "Wooden Wheels" in Chap. I.)

Steering Posts. The steering posts F and G can best be made on a lathe. Round off the top end of G and bore a 7/8-in. hole in the bottom end as shown in the drawing. Round off the lower end of F and bore a 7/8-in. hole at the top end. F and G may be fastened together with a tenon turned on F instead of with a dowel. Cut out a mortise 1 by 4 in. at the lower center part of steering post F with a saw and a chisel. In a similar manner, a mortise is cut at the upper part of G to receive the pony head.

Pony Head. On a piece of drawing paper or heavy wrapping paper 12 by 14 in., lay out 1-in. squares. This can best be done on a drawing board using the triangle and T square. Follow the outline of the pony's head in Plate 9. Notice where the curved line crosses each square. Locate the same points on your chart and connect these points with a free-hand line. When the pattern is of the desired shape, cut to the line carefully. Lay the pattern on the stock to be used and trace around it. With a coping saw or a turning saw cut the line and finish with a wood file and sandpaper.

Handle. The handle can be turned on a lathe or made from a piece of 7/8-in. dowel.

Assembling. The bolster E is fastened to the seat C, 2½ in. from the back with 1¾-in. No. 9 r.h. screws. Fasten the brace D to the seat C and to bolster E with 1¾-in. No. 9 f.h. screws. Connect the steering post G and the post F with a 7/8 by 4-in. dowel I, or with a 7/8-in. tenon turned on F. Use a black-iron washer between the posts G and the seat C, also between the posts F and C. These washers may be nailed to C with ½-in. box nails. The dowel I is held in place with 3/16 by 2-in. stove bolts. (See drawing.) The pony head is fastened to the steering post G with two

_____

(See directions for "Steering Posts" and "Assembling.") If you prefer to fasten F and G together with a 7/8-in. tenon turned on F, the stock for F will be 9¾ in. long.

HOBBY CAR

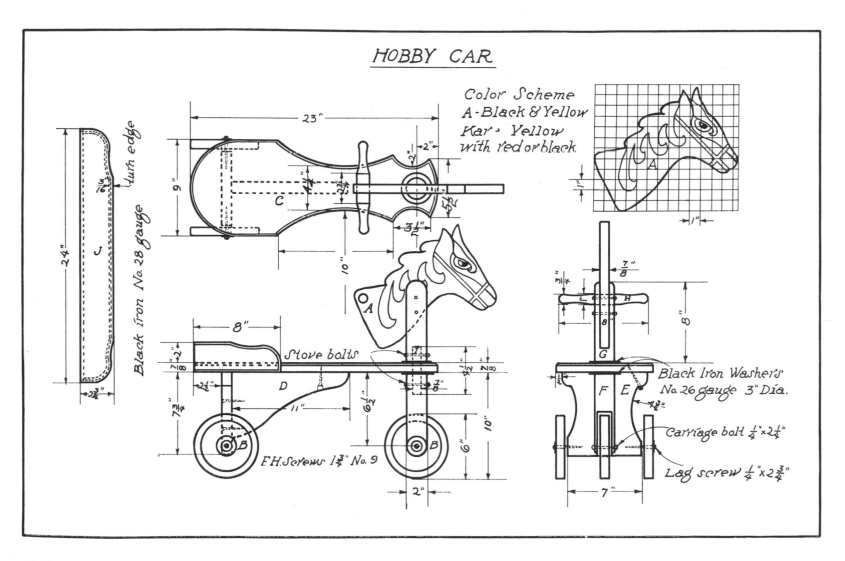

Color Scheme
A - Black & Yellow
Kar - Yellow
with red or black.

turn edge

Black iron No. 28 gauge

PLATE 9.   [Page 31]

³⁄₁₆ by 2-in. stove bolts. The back wheels are fastened to bolster E with ¼ by 2¾-in. lag bolts. Use washers between the bolt head and the wheel, also between the wheel and bolster E. The front wheel revolves on a carriage bolt ¼ by 2¾ in. The back piece J may be fastened to the back of seat C with ¾-in. box nails, or ¾-in. No. 7 r.h. screws.

Finishing. Enamel, oil stain, gloss paint, or lacquer may be used to finish this project. A suggested color scheme is given in Plate 9. Use a bright red, yellow, and black combination. Such parts as the outline of the head, the mane, the bridle, eyes, nostrils, and ears should be carefully trimmed in black. (See section on "Finishing and Coloring of Projects" in Chap. I.)

HOBBY CAR NO. 2

The Hobby Car illustrated in Plate 10 makes an excellent project for the general shop. It is simple in construction and well within the ability of the 9B and 9A student of junior-high-school age.

Bill of Material. Finished dimensions.

1 pc. ⅞ x 7 x 21   Seat (A) (Hardwood)
1 pc. ³⁄₁₆ x ¾ x 20   Bolster (B) (Band Iron)
1 pc. ³⁄₁₆ x ¾ x 11¼   Brace (C) (Band Iron)
1 pc. ³⁄₁₆ x ⅞ x 20   Fork (D) (Band Iron)
1 pc. ³⁄₁₆ x ⅞ x 3¼   Fork Connecting Part (J) (Band Iron)
1 pc. 1 in. diam. x 9   Handle (F)
1 pc. 2 in. diam. x 1¾   Block (G)
1 pc. ⅝ in. diam. x 14   Steering Rod (E) (Steel Rod)
1 pc. ⅜ in. diam. x 10¾   Back Axle (I) (Steel Rod)
1 pc. ⅜ in. diam. x 3   Front Axle (H) (Steel Rod)
3 Washers, 2 in. diam. x ⅛ in. thick
3 Wheels, 6½ in. diam., Double-Disc

Seat. Make the seat A of oak or birch. It is well to make a paper pattern first. Use heavy wrapping paper or drawing paper. Trace the pattern on the stock to be used. Cut to the line with a coping saw or a turning saw. Finish the seat smooth with a spokeshave, wood file, and sandpaper. Bore a ⅝-in. hole through the front end of A, 2 in. from the end. The handle F and the block G can be turned either on a lathe or made on the bench.

Bolster, Braces, Fork, etc. All the required band-iron parts can be cut with a hack saw. The holes should be located and drilled before bending any of the metal parts. The bend of all band-iron pieces in this project can be done cold. Follow the drawing carefully to get the shape of each part. The metal pieces can be held in a vise while the bending is being done. Use a hammer, mallet, monkey wrench, and a pair of pliers to bend or twist each band-iron piece to the proper shape.

Wheels. Double-disc iron wheels with rubber tires are suggested for this car. The wooden wheel illustrated in Plate 11 makes an excellent wheel also. (See section on "Double-Disc Wheels" in Chap. I.)

Assembling. Fasten the washers and block G to the front part of seat A with two ³⁄₁₆ by 3¼-in. rivets. The washers, and block G should be clamped to the front part of the seat A before drilling holes for the rivets. Countersink the rivets into the upper washer. (See section on "Drilling in Iron" in Chap. I.) The steering rod E is attached to fork D with a ³⁄₁₆ by 3½-in. rivet at the point Y shown in the drawing. Fasten the handle F to the steering rod with a ⅛ by 1-in. rivet. The bolster B may be fastened to the seat next. Attach piece B to seat A, 2¾ in. from the back end with two ³⁄₁₆ by 1½-in. f.h. stove bolts. The back axle fits through a hole in one end of the brace C and the other end of C

HOBBY CAR No. 2

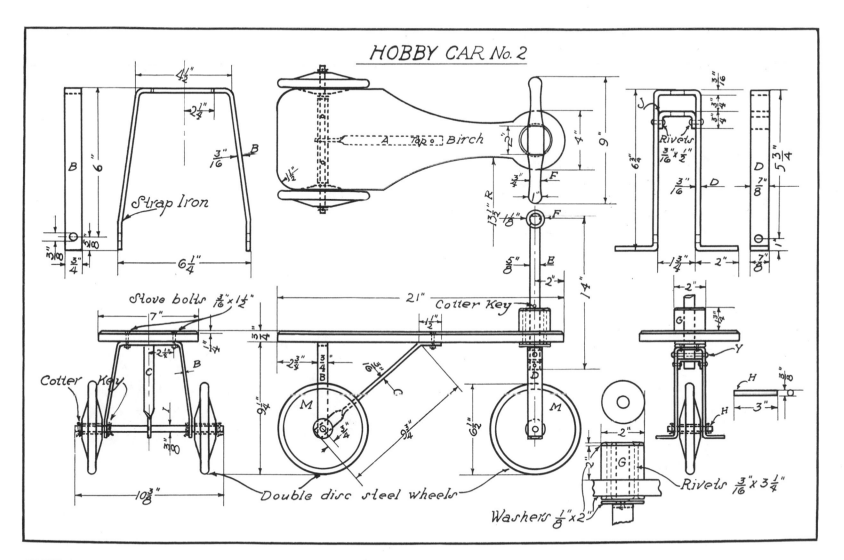

PLATE 10.

[Page 33]

is fastened to seat A with a ³⁄₁₆ by 1½-in. f.h. stove bolt. The legs of bolster B are kept in place with cotter keys, through the axle as indicated in Plate 10.

Finishing. A simple gloss paint, lacquer, or automobile enamel may be used to finish this project. Paint the seat, handle and wheels a bright red and all the metal parts, except the axles, black. (See section on "Finishing and Coloring of Projects" in Chap. I.)

KIDDOMOBILE

The Kiddomobile is a novel and very interesting project for a boy. The steering device and the auto hood on this project at once catch the youngsters' attention. The combination features make the project very interesting for pupils in 8A and 9B grades. It may be made in the home or in the school shop.

Bill of Material. Finished dimensions.

```
1 pc.    ⅞ x 9    x 28   Seat (A) (Hardwood)
1 pc.    ¾ x 6    x 12   Brace (B) (Hardwood)
1 pc.    ⅞ x 8    x  7   Bolster (C) (Hardwood)
1 pc.    ¾ x 4    x  8   Radiator Front (E) (Softwood)
1 pc.    ¾ x 4    x  9   Upright (F) (Softwood)
2 pc.    ½ x 1½ x  5   Spool Supports (J) (Hardwood)
1 pc.    ¾ x  4         Block (T)
1 pc.    2¾ x 21        Black Iron No. 28 Gauge, Back (N)
1 pc.   13    x 23½     Black Iron No. 28 Gauge, Hood
1 pc.    2½ in. diam. x 7¼  Steering Post (D) (Hardwood)
1 pc.    2½ in. diam. x 4   Cylinder (I)
1 pc.    1½ in. diam. x 3½  Steering Block (K)
1 pc.    1½ in. diam. x 2   Block (L)
1 pc.    1½ in. diam. x 1¼  Block (M)
1 pc.    ¾ in. diam. x 16   Steering Shaft (P)
1 pc.    ⅞ in. diam. x  6   Dowel (S)
1 Wheel, ¾ in. thick, 6 in. diam., Steering Wheel (G)
3 Wheels, 1¼ in. thick, 7 in. diam. (H)
2 Washers, 2½ in. diam., Black Iron, No. 26 Gauge
(See Pl. 11 and "Assembling" for hardware, etc.)
```

Seat. It is well to make a pattern of the seat A on paper first. Trace the pattern on the stock to be used. Cut to the line with a coping saw or a turning saw. Finish smooth with a spokeshave, wood file, and sandpaper. Bore a ⅞-in. hole through the front part of A, 2 in. from the end.

[Page 34]

Bolster, Braces, etc. Follow the directions and the details given in Plate 11 for shaping these pieces. Square these parts carefully. Mark out curved lines and cut to these lines with a coping saw or turning saw. Finish the edges with a spokeshave, wood file, and sandpaper.

FIG. 6. KIDDOMOBILE.

Wheels, Cylinder, etc. The wheels and the round parts of this project can best be made on a lathe. (See section on "Wooden

_____

If you prefer to fasten D and I with a tenon turned on D, the stock for D should be 10¼ in. long.

KIDDOMOBILE

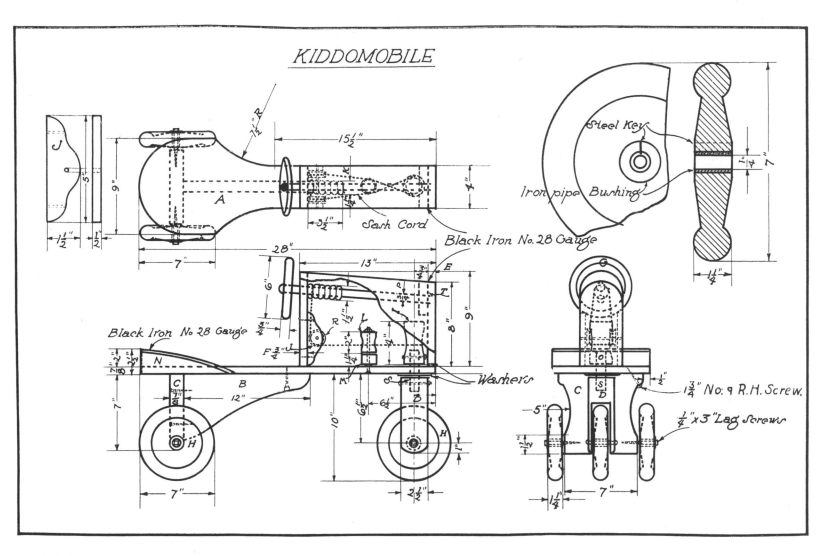

PLATE 11.

[Page 35]

Wheels" in Chap. I, and Pl. 11.) Any type of wooden wheel may be used. The steering post D is made 2½ in. in diameter and 7¼ in. long. Cut out a mortise 1⅜ by 5 in. at the lower center part of steering post D with a saw and a chisel. Bore a ⅞-in. hole at the top end to receive the connecting dowel S. Instead of using the dowel S, a tenon, ⅞ in. in diameter by 3 in. long may be turned on D. Bore a ⅞-in. hole at the lower end of cylinder I.

Assembling. The bolster C is fastened to seat A with 1¾-in. No. 9 r.h. screws. Fasten the brace B to seat A and to the bolster C with 1¾-in. No. 9 f.h. screws as shown in Plate 11. Attach the upright F to seat A, 13 in. from the front with 1¾-in. No. 9 f.h. screws. In like manner fasten the radiator front E to the front end of A. Nail the two black-iron washers at the top and bottom of A at the front end. Connect the cylinder I and the steering post D with a ⅞ by 4-in. dowel S. The dowel S is fastened to I and D with two ³⁄₁₆ by 2½-in. stove bolts as indicated in the drawing. The back wheels are fastened to bolster C with ¼ by 3-in. lag screws. Bore the hole slightly smaller than the thread of the screw before putting in the lag screws. Use a washer between the lag-screw head and the wheel, also between the wheel and the bolster C. The front wheel rotates on a carriage bolt ¼ by 2¾ in. Nail the block T to the radiator front E near the top end. Attach the steering shaft next. Nail the cylinder K to shaft P as shown in the drawing. Fasten the steering wheel on the end of the shaft. The supports J are fastened to the upright F with 1¼-in. No. 8 r.h. screws. The spools R revolve on a ¼ by 4-in. stove bolt as indicated in Plate 11. The cylinder L and the block M are held to seat A with a ¼ by 4-in. stove bolt. The block M is nailed to seat A leaving the cylinder L free to revolve. A sash cord or a seven-strand aerial wire may be used for the steering cable. Follow the details in Plate 11 for the proper location of the cable. The back piece N and the sheet-metal hood may be fastened to the car with ¾-in. escutcheon pins, box nails, or ¾-in. No. 6 r.h. screws.

Finishing. A simple gloss paint, lacquer, or enamel may be used to finish this project. A bright red color trimmed with yellow is suggested. (See section on "Finishing and Coloring of Projects" in Chap. I.)

BABY KAR

The Baby Kar illustrated in Plate 12 makes an ideal car for youngsters between the ages of 9 months and 3 years. It can be used as a walker at first and later as a hobby car. It also serves as an excellent cart for pulling baby about. A hardwood such as birch or oak should be used in making this project, but if it is not convenient to use hardwood, poplar may be used.

Bill of Material. Finished dimensions.

1 pc. ¾ x 5   x 15   Seat (A)
1 pc. ¾ x 10   x 12   Back Piece (B)
1 pc. ⅞ x 10   x 12¾   Front Part (C)

1 pc. ¾ x 1   x 15   Brace (F)
2 pc. ¾ x 1   x 16⅝   Sides of Frame (D)
2 pc. ¾ x 1   x 11½   Ends of Frame (E)
1 pc. ¾ x ¾   x 28   Tongue (G)
1 pc. ⅜ in. diam. x 3 Crosspiece (H)
2 Axles, ⅜ in. diam. x 5½ (J)
2 Wheels, 6½ in. diam., Double-Disc (K)
2 Casters, or Tea-Wagon Wheels
(See Pl. 12 and "Assembling" for hardware.)

Back, Front, Seat, and Brace. Square these parts carefully, and follow the directions and details for shaping as given in Plate 12. Mark out all curves and cut to the lines with a band saw, a

BABY KAR

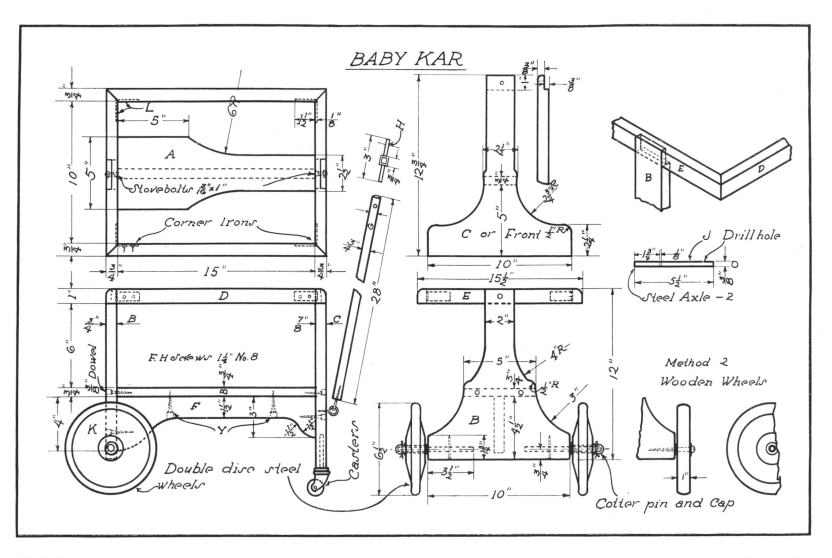

PLATE 12.

[Page 37]

coping saw, or a turning saw. Finish the edges with a spokeshave, wood file, and sandpaper. Cut a half lap at the top part of the back B and the front C. The length of the front C will depend on the kind of casters used for the front wheels.

Frame. Make the sides D of the frame ¾ in. thick, 1 in. wide, and 16⅝ in. long. Make the ends E, ¾ by 1 by 11½ in. Cut a half lap in the center of each end piece E.

Wheels. Double-disc steel wheels 6½ in. in diameter are recommended for this car. (See section on "Double-Disc Wheels" in Chap. I.) The wooden wheels illustrated in Plate 12, Method 2, are suitable for this project.

Assembling. Fasten brace F to seat A with 1¼-in. No. 8 f.h. screws as shown in the drawing. Fasten the front C and back B to the ends of F and A with 1¼-in. No. 8 f.h. screws. Set the heads of the screws halfway through the thickness of the wood. The heads of the screws and the holes may be covered with pieces of ⅜-in. dowel after the screws are inserted. Glue these in and plane them down smooth.

The frame is fastened together with glue and 1-in. brads and strengthened with corner irons. Chisel a groove in the frame ⅛ by ¾ by ½ in. on the inside of each piece before attaching the corner irons. Fasten the corner irons L to the frame with ½-in. No. 8 f.h. screws. The frame is attached to the front C and the back B by means of half-lap joints. The joints are held tight with glue and ³⁄₁₆ by 1-in. stove bolts. Rivet the ends of the bolts and file them smooth.

FIG. 7. BABY KAR.

Large screw eyes can be used to fasten the tongue G to the front of the car. Washers should be used between the back wheels and the back B.

Finishing. Enamel, oil stain, or gloss paint may be used to finish this project. (See section on "Finishing and Coloring of Projects" in Chap. I.) A bright red is suggested for the main color.

CHAPTER III
SCOOTERS AND WAGONS

A SCOOTUM

THE Scootum represents the popular homemade type of scooter for a boy. With a roller skate and a board or two at hand, almost any boy can construct this type of scooter. Any softwood will do for this project. White pine, basswood, or butternut are suggested.

Bill of Material. Finished dimensions.

1 pc. 1 x 3½ x 29 Baseboard (A)
1 pc. ¾ x 3½ x 28 Front Piece (B)
2 pc. ¾ x 3 x 20 Braces (C)
1 pc. ¾ x 2 x 12 Handle (D)
1 pc. ¾ x 2 x 3½ Block (E)
1 Roller Skate or 2 Ball-Bearing Casters

The details given in Plate 13 show clearly how the different parts of the Scootum are shaped and assembled.

Assembling. Fasten the front piece B to the front end of the base A with No. 10 finishing nails. Nail the braces C to the front piece B and to the sides of A with No. 8 finishing nails. The handle is attached to the top part of B with two $\frac{3}{16}$ by 2-in. stove bolts. Fasten the parts of a roller skate to the ends of base A with $\frac{3}{16}$ by 1½-in. stove bolts. Nail the block E to the front corner of A and B next. A metal shelf bracket may be used instead of the wooden braces C as shown in the drawing, Method 2.

Finishing. A water stain, oil stain, or simple gloss paint may be used to color and finish this Scootum. A red and blue combination is suggested. (See section on "Finishing and Coloring of Projects" in Chap. I.)

A SCOOTMOBILE

The Scootmobile illustrated in Plate 13 is a practical and a very interesting project for a boy. With the exception of the wheels, all wooden parts may be made of softwood. However, it is best to use hardwood such as birch or oak for every wooden part of the Scootmobile. If a softwood is used, poplar, white pine, or basswood are suggested.

Bill of Material. Finished dimensions.

1 pc. ⅞ x 4 x 23 Baseboard (A)
1 pc. ⅞ x 3 x 27 Front Piece (B)
1 pc. 1½ x 6½ x 6½ Connecting Block (C)
2 pc. ¾ x 3 x 8 Braces (D)
2 pc. ⅝ x 1¾ x 9¼ Sides of Back (E)
1 pc. ⅝ x ⅞ x 4 Back Piece (E)
1 pc. ⅜ in. diam. x 7½ Dowel-Rod Handle (F)
2 Wheels, ⅞ in. thick, 5-in. diam. (G)
1 Screen-Door Hinge (H)

Follow the details given in Plate 13 to get the shape of all the wooden parts. The front piece B, the connecting piece C, and the braces D may be laid out with a pair of dividers. Cut to the line with a coping saw or a turning saw and finish with a spokeshave, wood file, and sandpaper. The opening in the front piece B for the hinge can be cut by boring $\frac{1}{8}$-in. holes in a row. This can be finished with a $\frac{1}{8}$-in. chisel and a knife. The opening in the connecting block C may be cut with an ordinary ripsaw to the required depths.

Wheels. Nice wheels can be turned on a lathe. Use iron-pipe bushings for the wheels as illustrated in Plates 11 and 33. Very good wheels may also be cut at the bench with the use of a coping saw or a turning saw. (See section on "Wooden Wheels" in Chap. I.)

Assembling. Fasten the connecting block C to the front end of the baseboard A with $1\frac{3}{4}$-in. No. 9 f.h. screws. Fasten the braces D to the back end of A with $1\frac{3}{4}$-in. No. 9 r.h. screws. Nail the side and back pieces E with No. 6 finishing nails. Attach one half of the hinge H to the front piece B with two $\frac{3}{16}$ by $3\frac{1}{2}$-in. stove bolts. Fasten the other half of the hinge H to block C with $\frac{3}{16}$ by $1\frac{3}{4}$-in. stove bolts as shown in the drawing. Fasten the front wheel to the lower part of front piece B with a $\frac{1}{4}$ by $3\frac{1}{2}$-in. carriage bolt. Fasten the back wheel to the braces D with a $\frac{1}{4}$ by $3\frac{1}{2}$-in. carriage bolt also.

Finishing. An oil stain, outside paint, or enamel may be used to color and finish the Scootmobile. A red and blue color com-

FIG. 8. SCOOTUM AND SCOOTOMOBILE.

bination is suggested for this project. (See section on "Finishing and Coloring of Projects" in Chap. I.)

A SCOOTUM   A SCOOTMOBILE

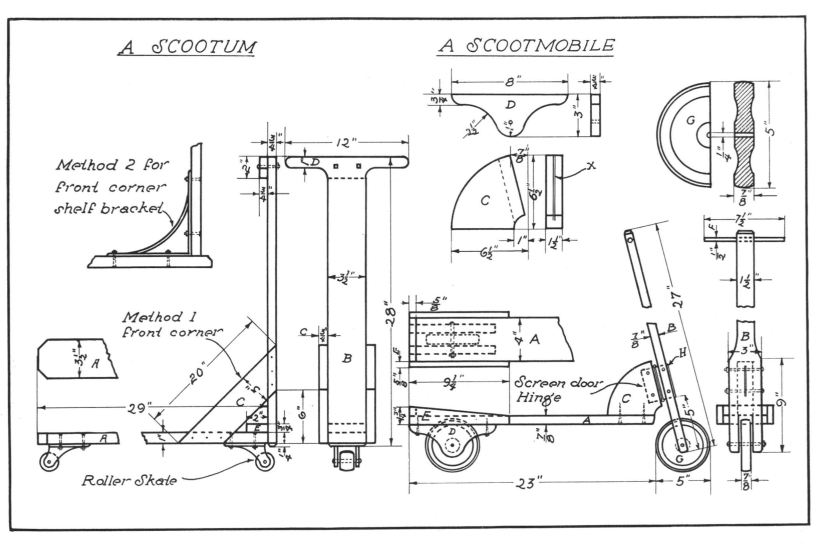

Method 2 for front corner shelf bracket

Method 1 front corner

20"

29"

Roller Skate

Screen door Hinge

PLATE 13.   [Page 41]

DELIVERSCOOT

The Deliverscoot illustrated in Plate 14 is a combined speed and delivery scooter. By taking off the box you have a typical boy scooter. Any softwood may be used in the construction of this project.

Bill of Material. Finished dimensions.

1 pc. $1\frac{1}{4}$ x 4 x 32 Baseboard (A)
1 pc. $\frac{3}{4}$ x 4 x 27 Front Piece (C)
2 pc. $\frac{5}{8}$ x 4 x 13 Braces (B)
1 pc. $1\frac{1}{4}$ x $1\frac{1}{2}$ x $4\frac{1}{2}$ Catch (I)
1 pc. $1\frac{1}{2}$ x 4 x 6 Triangle (H)
2 pc. $\frac{3}{4}$ x $\frac{3}{4}$ x 6 Cleats (E)
2 pc. $\frac{5}{8}$ x $9\frac{3}{8}$ x 14 Sides of Box (G)
2 pc. $\frac{5}{8}$ x $9\frac{3}{8}$ x 10 Ends of Box (G)
1 pc. $\frac{5}{8}$ x $11\frac{1}{4}$ x 14 Bottom of Box (G)
1 pc. $\frac{3}{8}$ in. diam. x $4\frac{1}{2}$ Dowel Crosspiece (D)
1 pc. $2\frac{1}{2}$ x 18 Black Iron No. 28 Gauge, Back (F)

Roller skates or ball-bearing casters may be used for the wheels of this scooter. Follow the details in Plate 14 to get the shape of all parts. An ordinary grocery box may be used instead of the one suggested in the drawing.

Assembling. Fasten the front piece C to the base A, 6 in. from the front end with 2-in. No. 9 f.h. screws. Cut in notches on each side of C, $\frac{5}{8}$ in. deep, to receive the braces B before inserting the screws. In like manner, notches should be cut on each side of the base A $\frac{5}{8}$ by $4\frac{3}{4}$ in. as shown in the drawing. Fasten the braces B to the edges of A and C, where notches are cut, with $1\frac{1}{4}$-in. No. 8 f.h. screws. Attach the roller-skate parts to each end of base A next. Use $\frac{3}{16}$ by $1\frac{1}{2}$-in. f.h. stove bolts. Nail the wedge block H to the front part of base A. The top edge of the black-iron back F should be turned before it is attached to A. Nail this part to the back end of base A with $\frac{3}{4}$-in. box nails. Assemble the box G with glue and 2-in. brads. The box is held to the front part of the scooter with a catch I, a dowel at the center, and cleats E nailed under the box.

Finishing. A stain, paint, or enamel may be used to color and finish the Deliverscoot. (See section on "Finishing and Coloring of Projects" in Chap. I.)

DELIVERSCOOT

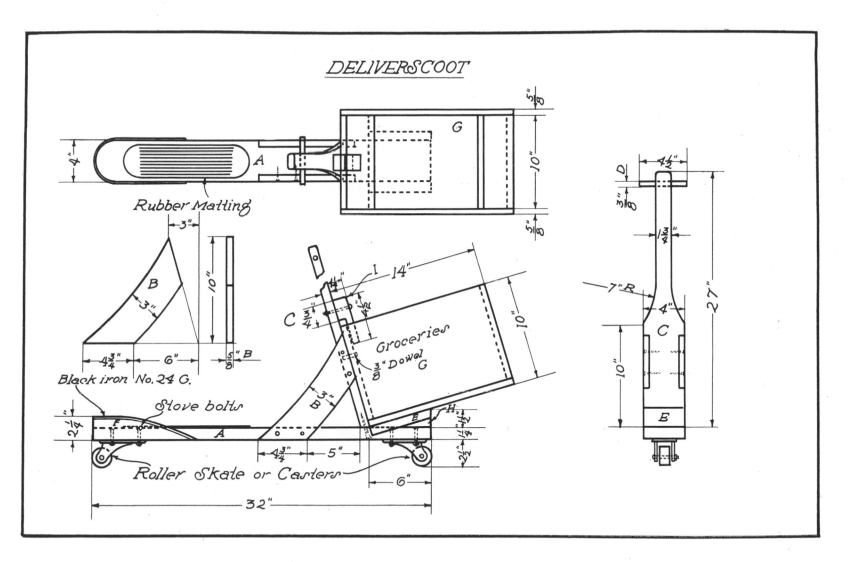

Rubber Matting

Black iron No. 24 G.

Stove bolts

Roller Skate or Casters

Groceries

$\frac{3}{8}$" Dowel

PLATE 14.   [Page 43]

A SCOOTER

The Scooter illustrated in Plate 15 is a very interesting project involving a combination of materials and operations. It is well within the ability of the 8A and 9B students of the junior high school. Use hardwood for all wooden parts on this project. Birch or oak are very good. Band iron is used for the metal parts. The bending of band-iron parts can be easily done cold.

Bill of Material. Finished dimensions.

1 pc. ⅞ x 5   x 23   Baseboard (A)
1 pc. 1   x 1½ x 19   Front Piece (C)
1 pc. ¾ x ¾ x 6½ Block (K)
2 pc. ³⁄₁₆ x ¾ x 12   Front Irons (D)
2 pc. ³⁄₁₆ x ¾ x 10   Back Irons (J)
1 pc. ¼ x ¾ x 13   Connecting Iron (G)
1 pc. ¼ x ¾ x 16¼ Connecting Iron (H)
1 pc. ³⁄₁₆ x ¾ x 5½ Pivot Iron (E)
2 pc. ³⁄₁₆ x ¾ x 3   Corner Irons (I)
1 pc. 1⅛ in. diam. x 9   Handle (R)
1 Axle, ⅜ in. diam. x 6   Back Axle
1 Axle, ⅜ in. diam. x 3½ Front Axle
1 Bolt, ¼ in. diam. x 4½ Pivot Bolt (F)
1 doz. ³⁄₁₆ by 1½-in. Rivets and a few ³⁄₁₆ by 2-in. Rivets
2 Wheels, 8½ in. diam., Double-Disc (B)

Base, Front, and Handle. Lay out the baseboard A according to details given in Plate 15. Use a coping saw to cut out the opening for the back wheel. Bore a ⅜-in. hole for the back axle 2 in. from the back. Cut places on each side of A, ³⁄₁₆ in. deep to receive the back irons J. Make the front piece 1 by 1½ in. at the lower end and 1 by 1 in. at the upper part. The handle R can be made by hand or turned on a lathe.

Band-Iron Parts. All band-iron parts can be cut to the required lengths with a hack saw. Locate and drill all holes before bending any of the metal parts. (See section on "Drilling in Iron" in Chap. I.) With the use of a vise, hammer, monkey wrench, and a pair of pliers, it is a small matter to bend the different parts to the required shape.

FIG. 9. SCOOTER.

Wheels. Double-disc steel wheels 8½ in. in diameter are suggested for this Scooter. (See section on "Double-Disc Wheels" in Chap. I.)

A SCOOTER

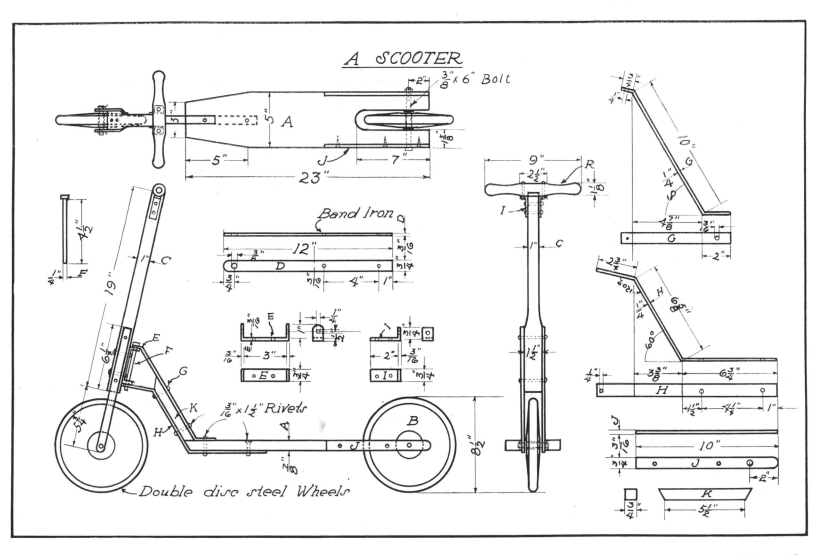

Band Iron

Double disc steel Wheels

PLATE 15.

[Page 45]

Assembling. Fasten the back irons J to baseboard A with 1-in. No. 8 f.h. screws. Bore small holes in the wood and countersink the holes in the irons before inserting the screws. Fasten the connecting braces G and H to block K with $\frac{3}{16}$ by 1½-in. rivets. Attach the lower ends of braces G and H to the front of baseboard A with $\frac{3}{16}$ by 1½-in. rivets. Fasten the two front irons D to the lower part of the front piece G with $\frac{3}{16}$ by 2½-in. rivets. Attach the handle R to the top end of C with the corner irons I. Use $\frac{3}{16}$ by 1½-in. rivets to hold these parts together. The pivot iron E is fastened to the front piece C, 1 in. from each end of E, with $\frac{3}{16}$ by 1½-in. rivets. Use washers on the rivets next to the wood. Connect the top ends of the connecting braces G and H to the pivot iron E with a ¼ by 4½-in. machine bolt F. The bolt is held in place by means of a cotter key. Attach the wheels and the axles next. Place washers between the wheels and the irons. Insert cotter keys through the ends of the axles to hold the wheels in place.

Finishing. Take the wheels off, and detach the Scooter at the pivot E to finish this project. A gloss paint, lacquer, or enamel may be used in coloring and finishing the Scooter. (See section on "Finishing and Coloring of Projects" in Chap. I.) Paint or enamel all band-iron parts black. Finish and color the wooden parts and the wheels a bright red.

BOY SCOOTER

The Boy Scooter is a novel and very interesting project. The combination of materials and the novelty features of this project are sure to make a striking appeal to every boy. It makes an excellent newspaper carrier for the busy newsboy. With a box attached to the top, it can also be used for delivering. With the exception of the base A and the handle R, any softwood may be used for the wooden parts of the Boy Scooter. Make the baseboard A and the handle R of hardwood. Band iron is used for the metal parts.

Bill of Material. Finished dimensions.

1 pc.	¾ x 5 x 26	Baseboard	(A)
1 pc.	¾ x 12 x 18	Top	(B)
1 pc.	¾ x 5 x 12	Brace	(E)
1 pc.	¾ x 7 x 5	Brace	(C)
1 pc.	1 x 6½ x 11½	Bolster	(D)
1 pc.	¾ x ¾ x 7½	Block	(O)
1 pc.	¼ x ¾ x 15¼	Iron Connecting Brace	(J)
1 pc.	¼ x ¾ x 16¾	Iron Connecting Brace	(K)
2 pc.	$\frac{3}{16}$ x ¾ x 26	Fork Irons	(G)
2 pc.	$\frac{3}{16}$ x ¾ x 4	Pivot Irons	(H)
1 pc.	1⅛ in. diam. x 9	Handle	(R)
1 Bolt,	¼ in. diam. x 5¼	Machine Bolt	(I)
2 Axles,	⅜ in. diam. x 5½		
3 Wheels,	8½ in. diam., Double-Disc		(N)

Lay out all wooden parts such as the base A, top B, brace E, bolster D, handle R, and block O according to the details given in Plate 17. All band-iron parts can be cut to the required lengths with a hack saw. Locate and drill all holes before bending any of the metal parts. (See section on "Drilling in Iron" in Chap. I.) With the use of a vise, hammer, monkey wrench, and a pair of pliers it is a small matter to bend the metal parts to the required shape.

Wheels. Double-disc steel wheels 8½ in. in diameter are suggested for this scooter. (See section on "Double-Disc Wheels" in Chap. I.)

Assembling. Fasten the baseboard A to the braces C and E and to bolster D with 1½-in. No. 9 f.h. screws as shown in

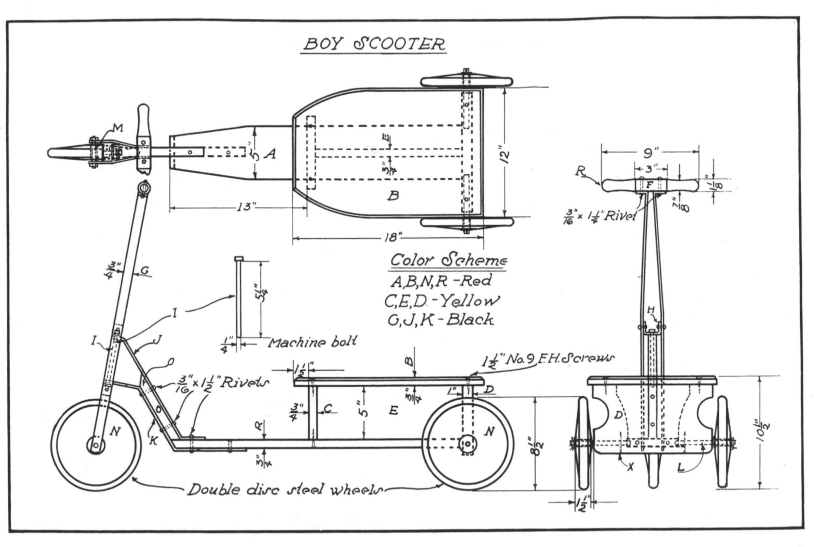

BOY SCOOTER

Color Scheme

A,B,N,R – Red
C,E,D – Yellow
G,J,K – Black

Machine bolt

$\frac{3}{16}'' \times 1\frac{1}{2}''$ Rivets

$1\frac{1}{2}''$ No.9 F.H. Screws

$\frac{3}{16}'' \times 1\frac{1}{4}''$ Rivet

Double disc steel wheels

PLATE 16.

[Page 47]

DETAILS OF BOY SCOOTER

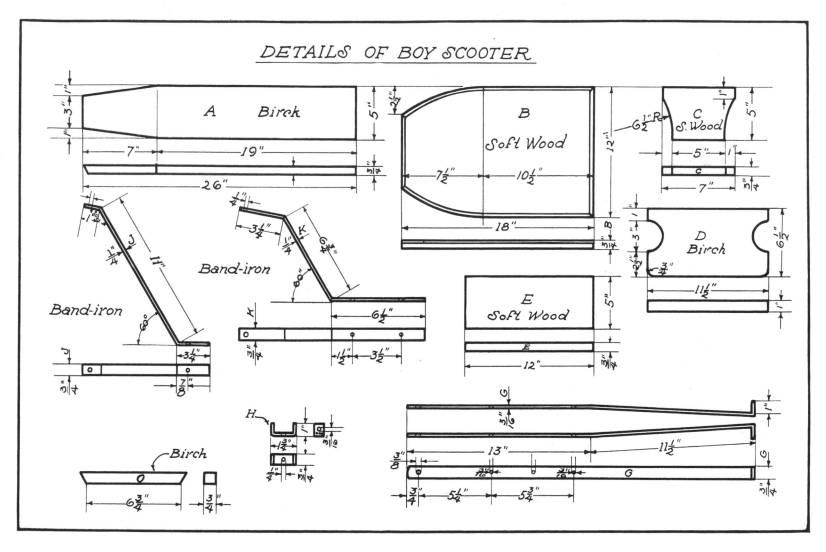

PLATE 17.

JUNIOR WAGON

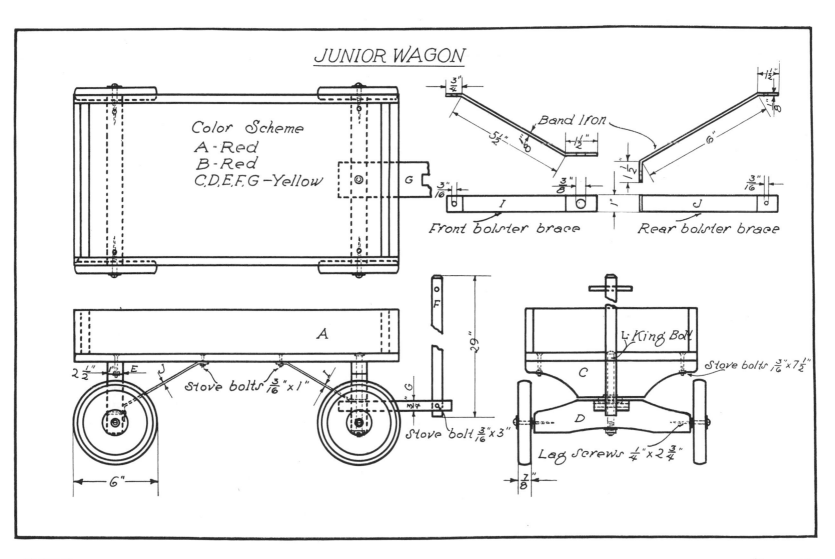

Color Scheme
A - Red
B - Red
C, D, E, F, G - Yellow

Band Iron

Front bolster brace

Rear bolster brace

L - King Bolt

Stove bolts $\frac{3}{16}" \times 7\frac{1}{2}"$

Lag screws $\frac{1}{4}" \times 2\frac{3}{4}"$

Stove bolts $\frac{3}{16}" \times 1"$

Stove bolt $\frac{3}{16}" \times 3"$

PLATE 18.

[Page 49]

Plate 16. Fasten the top B to parts C, E, and D with 1½-in No. 9 f.h. screws. Fasten the connecting braces J and K to the block O with ³⁄₁₆ by 1½-in. rivets. Attach the lower ends of J and K to the front part of base A with ³⁄₁₆ by 1½-in. rivets. Connect the fork irons G to the pivot irons H. Use ³⁄₁₆ by ½-in. rivets to fasten the pivot irons to the fork G. Fasten the handle R to the top of the fork irons with ³⁄₁₆ by 1½-in. rivets. Connect the top ends of the connecting braces J and K to the pivot irons H of the fork with a 1¼ by 5¼-in. machine bolt I. Drive back the axles L into the bolster D. Drill ⅛-in. holes at the point X through the bottom edge of D and through the axles as shown in Plate 16. Place washers between the wheels and the bolster, and between the front wheel and the irons. Insert cotter keys through the ends of the axles to hold the wheels in place.

Finishing. Take the wheels off and detach the Boy Scooter at the pivot irons H to finish the project. A gloss paint, oil stain, lacquer, or enamel may be used in coloring and finishing. The iron parts should be either painted or enameled. A color scheme is given in the drawing, Plate 16. (See section on "Coloring and Finishing of Projects" in Chap. I.)

JUNIOR WAGON

The Junior Wagon illustrated in Plates 18 and 19 has always been a very interesting project. It is, without doubt, every youngster's best friend. With the exception of the wheels, all wooden parts may be constructed of softwood. It is best, however, to use hardwood for such parts as the front bolster C, the rear bolster E, and the tongue F. A hardwood should be used for the wheels.

Bill of Material. Finished dimensions.
2 pc. ⅝ x 3⅛ x 23   Sides of Box (A)
2 pc. ⅝ x 3⅛ x 10¾ Ends of Box (A)
1 pc. ⅝ x 12 x 23 Bottom of Box (A)
1 pc. 1 x 2⅝ x 12 Top Front Bolster (C)
1 pc. 1 x 2⅝ x 11⅜ Bottom Front Bolster (D)
1 pc. 1 x 5½ x 11⅜ Rear Bolster (E)
1 pc. ¾ x ¾ x 29   Tongue (F)
1 pc. ¾ x 2½ x 8   Tongue Brace (G)
1 pc. ⅛ x 1 x 7¾   Front Bolster Brace (I) (Band Iron)
1 pc. ⅛ x 1 x 8¼   Rear Bolster Brace (J) (Band Iron)
1 pc. ⅜ in. diam. x 3 Dowel (H)
2 Washers, ⅛ x 2 in. diam. (K)
1 Carriage Bolt, ⅜ in. diam. x 5½ Kingbolt (L)
2 Wheels, ⅞ in. thick, 6 in. diam. (B)
(See Pl. 18 and "Assembling" for hardware.)

Bolsters. Follow the details given in Plate 19 for shaping these parts. Square the stock for the bolsters carefully. Mark out curved lines and cut to these lines with a coping saw or a turning saw. Finish the edges with a spokeshave, wood file, and sandpaper.

Iron Braces. Band iron is used for the bolster braces. Locate and drill all holes before bending the ends of these pieces. (See section on "Drilling in Iron" in Chap. I.) The braces may be held in a vise while the ends are being bent to the proper angles.

Wheels. The wheels for this project can best be made on a lathe. However, if a turning lathe is not available, neat wheels may be cut with the use of a coping saw. A good wheel with a pipe bushing is illustrated in Plate 11. (See section on "Wooden Wheels" in Chap. I.)

Assembling. Assemble the box A with glue and 2-in. finishing nails. Fasten the back bolster E and the front top bolster C to the box of the wagon with ³⁄₁₆ by 1½-in. stove bolts as shown in Plate 18. The iron bolster braces may be attached to the wagon next. Use ³⁄₁₆ by 1-in. stove bolts to attach the iron braces to the box A. The back end of the iron brace J is fastened to bolster E

DETAILS of JUNIOR WAGON

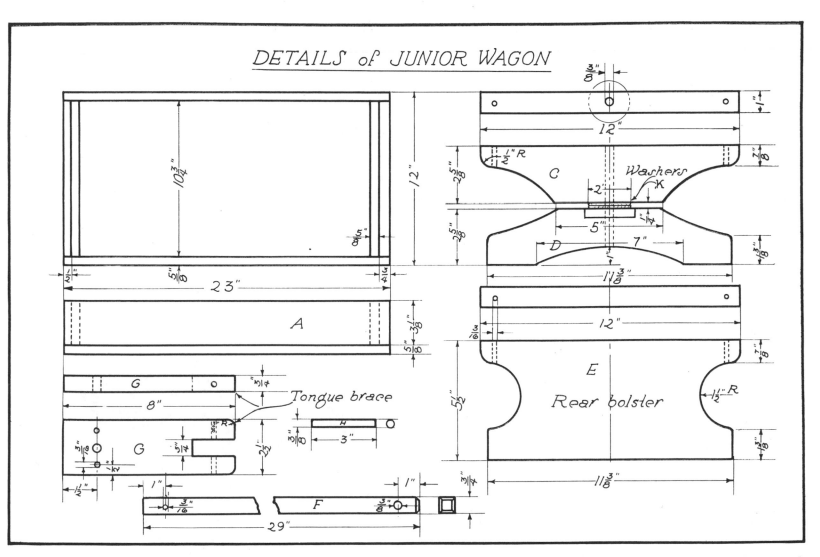

PLATE 19.

[Page 51]

with a $\frac{3}{16}$ by $1\frac{1}{4}$-in. stove bolt. The front end of the iron brace I is held in place by the kingbolt L. Fasten the tongue brace G to the lower front bolster with a $1\frac{1}{2}$-in. No. 8 f.h. screw. Fasten the wheels to holsters D and E with $\frac{1}{4}$ by $2\frac{3}{4}$-in. lag screws. Place washers between the screw heads and the wheels, also between the wheels and bolsters. Attach the lower front bolster to the top bolster with a $\frac{1}{2}$ by $5\frac{1}{2}$-in. carriage bolt (kingbolt). Use two washers $\frac{1}{8}$ by 2-in. in diameter between C and D. The tongue is fastened to the tongue brace G with a $\frac{3}{16}$ by 3-in. stove bolt.

Finishing. A gloss paint, water or oil stain, or enamel may be used in coloring and finishing the Junior Wagon. A color scheme is given in Plate 18. (See section on "Coloring and Finishing of Projects" in Chap. I.)

COASTER WAGON

Every boy between 9 and 15 years of age likes to be the proud possessor of a coaster wagon, particularly one that he has built himself. The Coaster Wagon illustrated in Plates 20 and 21 is of the ordinary type and well within the ability of the 8A or 9B student. Any softwood such as butternut or pine may be used for the box part, although the box will be more substantial if made of hardwood. The bolsters E, C, D, and the tongue F should be made of hardwood such as birch or oak.

Bill of Material. Finished dimensions.

2 pc. $\frac{1}{2}$ x $3\frac{1}{4}$ x 37   Sides of Box (A)
2 pc. $\frac{5}{8}$ x $3\frac{1}{4}$ x 13   Ends of Box (A)
1 pc. $\frac{1}{2}$ x $2\frac{1}{2}$ x 15   Front Top Piece (A)
1 pc. $\frac{1}{2}$ x 1   x 15   Back End of Frame
2 pc. $\frac{1}{2}$ x 1   x 38   Sides of Box Frame
1 pc. $\frac{1}{2}$ x 15   x 38   Bottom of (A)
4 pc. $\frac{5}{8}$ x $1\frac{3}{4}$ x 15   Crosspieces (S)
1 pc. $1\frac{1}{4}$ x $5\frac{3}{4}$ x 13   Rear Bolster (E)
2 pc. $1\frac{1}{4}$ x $2\frac{3}{4}$ x 13   Front Bolsters (C) and (D)
1 pc. $\frac{7}{8}$ x $\frac{7}{8}$ x 20   Tongue (F)
1 pc. $\frac{1}{8}$ x $\frac{3}{4}$ x 12   Iron Brace (J)
1 pc. $\frac{1}{8}$ x $\frac{3}{4}$ x $11\frac{3}{4}$ Iron Brace (I)
1 pc. $\frac{1}{8}$ x $\frac{3}{4}$ x 12   Tongue Brace (K)
1 pc. $\frac{1}{8}$ x 1   x 29   Tongue Connection (G)
2 pc. $\frac{1}{8}$ x $\frac{3}{4}$ x 6   Tongue Irons (L)
(See Pl. 21 and "Assembling" for hardware.)

Bolsters. Follow the details given in Plate 21 for shaping these parts. Square the stock for the bolsters carefully. Mark out curved lines, and cut to these lines with a band saw or a coping saw. Finish the curved edges with a spokeshave, wood file, and sandpaper. With a $\frac{1}{2}$-in. gouge cut a groove at the bottom edge of the back bolster E and the lower front bolster D to receive the axles.

FIG. 10. COASTER WAGON.

Iron Braces, etc. Band iron is used for all necessary flat iron parts. All metal parts can be cut to the required length with a hack saw. Locate and drill all holes before bending any of the

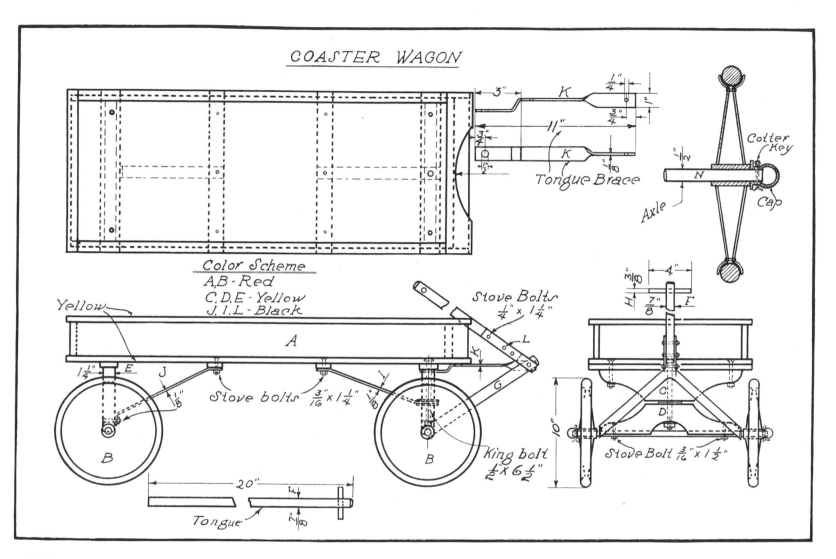

COASTER WAGON

Color Scheme
A,B - Red
C,D,E - Yellow
J,I,L - Black

Tongue Brace

Cotter Key

Axle

N

Cap

Yellow

Stove Bolts ¼" x 1¼"

A

L

E

J

Stove bolts 3/16" x 1¼"

King bolt ½" x 6½"

Stove Bolt 3/16" x 1½"

B

B

G

Tongue

20"

PLATE 20. [Page 53]

band-iron parts. (See section on "Drilling in Iron" in Chap. I.) The bending of the iron parts can be easily done cold. (See detailed drawing, Pl. 21.)

Wheels. Double-disc wheels 8½ or 10 in. in diameter are recommended for this wagon. The axles may be purchased to fit the wheels. (See section on "Double-Disc Wheels" in Chap. I.)

Assembling. The box A can be assembled with glue and 2-in. brads, or 1½-in. No. 8 r.h. screws can be used for the sides, and 1¼-in. No. 8 f.h. screws for the bottom. The frame is nailed to the edge of the box with 1¾- or 2-in. brads. The crosspieces S are fastened to the under part of box A with 1¼-in. No. 8 f.h. screws. The axles are attached to the bolsters with ¼ by 1½-in. carriage bolts as shown in Plate 20. Slip on the tongue-connection piece before bolting the front axle to the bolster. Fasten the back bolster E and the front top bolster C to the crosspieces and to box A with ¼ by 2½-in. carriage bolts. The rear bolster brace J is fastened to the body and back bolster with $\frac{3}{16}$ by 1¼-in. stove bolts. The front end of the brace I is held in place by the kingbolt. Attach the front bolster D to the bolster C and the body A with a ½ by 6½-in. carriage bolt (kingbolt). The wheels are held in place by means of cotter keys and caps. (See details, Pl. 21.) The tongue brace K and the tongue may be added next. Use ¼ by 1¼-in. carriage bolts to fasten the irons L to the tongue F. The tongue, tongue brace, and tongue connection are held together with a ¼ by 1¼-in. carriage bolt. One end of the tongue brace is fastened to the king bolt. A ⅜ by 4-in. dowel can be used for the crosspiece of the tongue.

Finishing. A gloss paint, water or oil stain, or enamel may be used in coloring and finishing the Coaster Wagon. A color scheme is given in Plate 20. (See section on "Coloring and Finishing of Projects" in Chap. I.)

DETAILS OF COASTER WAGON

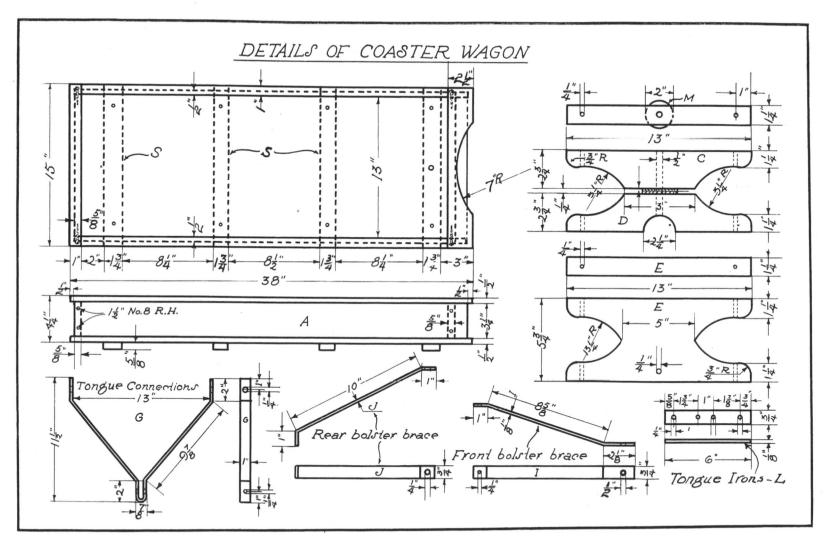

PLATE 21.

[Page 55]

CHAPTER IV

PUSHMOBILES

THE "FLYER" PUSHMOBILE

THE "Flyer" Pushmobile is simple in construction, yet very substantial and is built light for speed. The wooden parts of the "Flyer" can be made of softwood such as pine or butternut.

Bill of Material. Finished dimensions.
```
1 pc.  ¾ x 4 x 57¼   Baseboard (A)
1 pc.  ¾ x 4 x 17    Cowl Piece (B)
1 pc.  ¾ x 4 x 16¾   Radiator Board (C)
2 pc.  ¾ x 6 x 12    Seat Braces (D)
1 pc.  ⅞ x 7 x 12    Back (E)
1 pc.  ¾ x 7 x 10    Bottom of Seat (F)
1 pc. 1¾ x 3 x 11    Back Bolster (G)
1 pc. 1⅜ x 3 x  7    Top Front Bolster (I)
1 pc. 1⅜ x 3 x 11    Lower Front Bolster (H)
1 pc.  ¾ x 2 x 11    Foot Rest (J)
1 pc.  ¾ x 2 x  4    Brace (R)
1 pc. 1½ x 4 x  4    Block (U)
1 pc. 25 x 43 Black Iron No. 28 Gauge, Hood
1 pc. 1¾ in. diam. x 4  Cylinder (L)
1 Mopstick, 32 in. long, Steering Shaft (K)
1 Steering Wheel (auto or coaster-wagon wheel) (M)
4 Wheels (coaster-wagon wheels or baby-buggy wheels)
2 Axles, ½ x 16 (to fit wheels)
1 Sash Cord, 60 in. long.
2 Pulleys, for guides in steering device
(See drawings and "Assembling" for hardware.)
```

Bolsters, and Braces. Follow the details given in Plate 22 for shaping these parts. Square the stock for the bolsters carefully. Cut notches in the lower part of the bolsters G, H, and I to allow for the bolt heads. With a ½-in. gouge, or a gouge the width of the axles, cut grooves into the bottom edges of G and H for the axles. Bore all necessary holes. Round off the top ends of B and C with a coping saw, spokeshave, file, and sandpaper.

Steering Device. Use a mopstick or a broomstick for the steering shaft K. If a lathe is not available for shaping the cylinder L, a large spool may be used, or a cylinder can be shaped on the bench with the use of a plane and a spokeshave. A coaster-wagon wheel, a wooden wheel turned on a lathe, or an old discarded auto steering wheel may be used for the steering wheel.

Wheels, and Axles. Coaster-wagon wheels or baby-buggy wheels may be used for this pushmobile. Use axles that will fit the wheels. (See section on "Double-Disc Wheels" in Chap. I.)

Assembling. The radiator piece C is nailed to the front end of base A with No. 8 finishing nails. The upright B is fastened to base A, 25 in. from the front, with No. 8 finishing nails. Nail the brace R to A and B next. The pieces D, E, and F are nailed together and then nailed to base A forming the seat, as shown in Plate 22.

Fasten the bolster G to the back end of base A with ½ by 4½-in. carriage bolts. Fasten the front top bolster I to the front end of base A with ⅜ by 3½-in. carriage bolts. (See details in Pl. 22.) Attach the lower bolster H to I and A with a ½ by 5-in. carriage bolt (kingbolt P). Use two large washers between I and

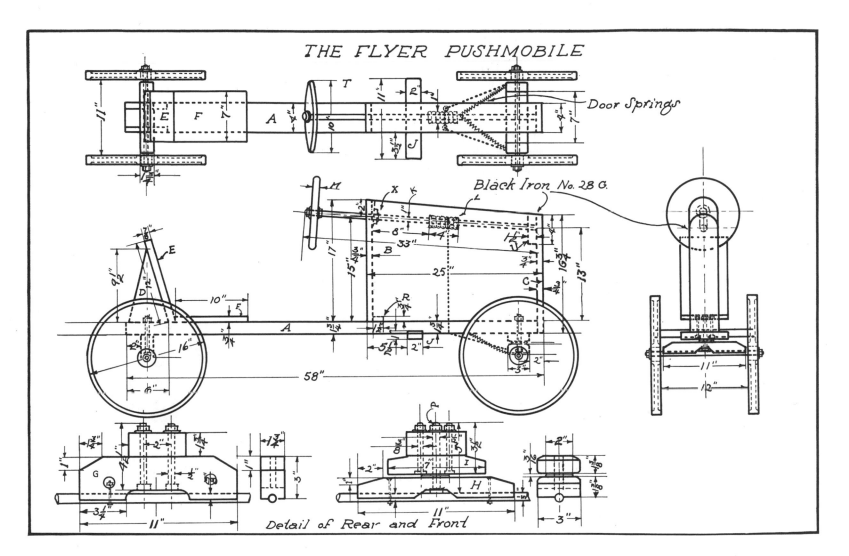

THE FLYER PUSHMOBILE

Door Springs

Black Iron No. 28 G.

Detail of Rear and Front

PLATE 22.

[Page 57]

H. The axles are fastened to the back bolster G and the lower front bolster H with $\frac{3}{16}$ by 2-in. stove bolts. The wheels are held in place with cotter keys inserted through the ends of each axle. Use washers between the wheels and the bolsters, also between the cotter keys and the wheels.

Attach the steering shaft K next. Nail the cylinder L to the shaft K at the center. One end of the shaft K fits in the block U. The steering shaft is held in place by a large metal or galvanized-iron washer and a cotter key. The key is placed through the shaft at the point X. A piece of sash cord makes an excellent steering cable. Wind this cable around the cylinder L, carry it through the holes in part A, and fasten the ends to large screw eyes at each side of the front bolster H. Screen-door springs may be used to keep the front wheels steady while steering the car.

Finishing. A simple gloss paint is suggested to color and finish this pushmobile. A navy blue trimmed with gray, or any color combination to suit the owner's taste may be used. (See section on "Finishing and Coloring of Projects" in Chap. I.)

THE RAMBLER

In the Rambler we have another suggestive type of pushmobile. A boy may use his own initiative and ingenuity in adding more to this model such as headlights, bumpers, or any other accessories. A light-weight softwood, such as butternut, pine, or basswood, may be used to build the framework of this car.

Bill of Material. Finished dimensions.
1 pc. $\frac{3}{4}$ x 9   x 12 Seat Back (A)
1 pc. $\frac{7}{8}$ x 9   x 17 Part (B)
1 pc. $\frac{7}{8}$ x 6   x 15 Radiator Board (C)
2 pc. $\frac{7}{8}$ x 12 x 21 Back Pieces (F)
1 pc. $\frac{7}{8}$ x $12\frac{1}{2}$ x 70 Baseboard (G)
1 pc. $1\frac{3}{4}$ x 5   x 13 Front Brace (D)
1 pc. $\frac{3}{4}$ x 3   x 15 Foot Rest (P)
1 pc. $1\frac{1}{4}$ x $3\frac{1}{2}$ x 6 Guide Block (H)
1 pc. $\frac{3}{4}$ x 6   x 9 Wedge-Shaped Piece (K)
2 pc. $\frac{3}{4}$ x $1\frac{1}{2}$ x 19 Sides of Handle (M)
1 pc. $\frac{3}{4}$ x $1\frac{3}{4}$ x 13 Crosspiece of Handle (N)
2 pc. 1   x $1\frac{1}{2}$ x 60 Rubber Hose (J)
1 pc. $2\frac{1}{2}$ in. diam. x 4 Steering Cylinder (E)
6 pc. $\frac{7}{8}$ in. diam. x 1 Exhaust-Pipe Supports (I)
1 Mopstick, $\frac{3}{4}$ x 33, Steering Shaft (L)
1 Steering Wheel (auto or coaster-wagon wheel)
2 Window-Sash Pulleys (to guide steering cable)
1 pc. Sash Cord, 6 ft. long
1 bundle of Lath (for hood and top of back)
(See Plates 23 and 24 and "Assembling" for hardware, wheels, etc.)

FIG. 11. THE RAMBLER.

Framework. Follow the details given in Plate 24 for shaping all the wooden parts. Lay out the curves in parts C, B, and F with a pair of dividers. Cut to the line with a coping saw or a turning saw and finish with a spokeshave, wood file, and sandpaper. Make part K wedge shape as shown in the detailed drawing.

THE RAMBLER

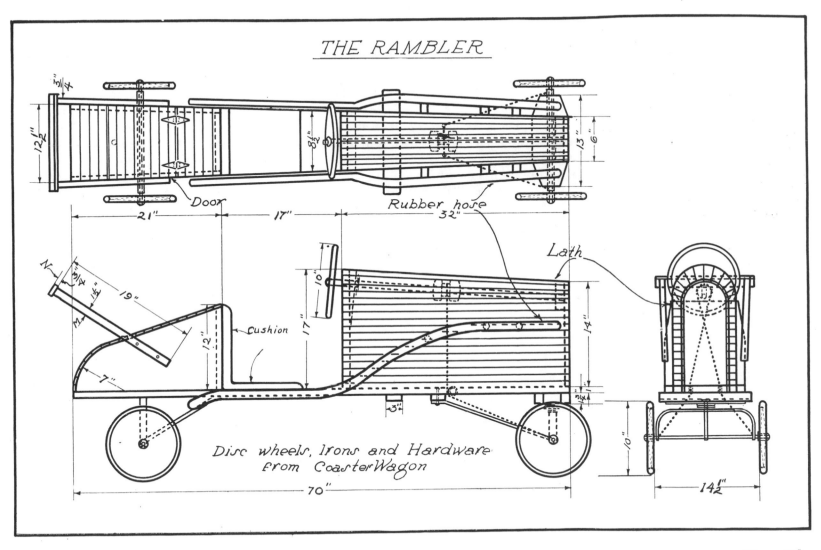

Door

Rubber hose

Lath

Cushion

Disc wheels, Irons and Hardware from Coaster Wagon

PLATE 23.

[Page 59]

Steering Device. Use a mopstick or a broomstick for the steering shaft G. If a lathe is not available for turning out the steering cylinder E, a large spool may be used, or a cylinder may be shaped on the bench with the use of a plane, spokeshave, saw, and chisel. A coaster-wagon wheel, a wooden wheel turned on a lathe, or an old discarded auto steering wheel may be used for the steering wheel on the Rambler. A sash cord or an aerial wire makes an excellent steering cable. Window-sash pulleys or other small pulleys work nicely for the cable guides.

Wheels and Axles. Wheels, irons, and hardware from a coaster wagon may be used on the Rambler. (See section on "Double-Disc Wheels" in Chap. I.)

Assembling. The seat back A, part B, the radiator board C, and the back pieces F are fastened to the baseboard G with 1¾-in. No. 9 f.h. screws as shown in Plate 24. Nail the block H to part of C and the wedge block K to the top part of B. Attach the steering shaft L next. Nail the cylinder E to the shaft L at the center. One end of the shaft L fits in the block H. The steering shaft is held in place by a large metal washer and a cotter key. The key is placed through the shaft at the point X.

Wind the cable around cylinder E, carrying through the pulleys in baseboard G, and fasten the ends to each side of the front bolster. The front brace D is fastened to the front end of baseboard G with 1¾-in. No. 9 f.h. screws. The block supports for the exhaust pipe can be fastened to the car with 1½-in. No. 9 f.h. screws. Attach the exhaust-pipe hose to the blocks I with wire or nail it to the blocks. The back and front bolsters and the braces are fastened to the baseboard G with stove bolts.

Finishing. An outside gloss paint is suggested to color and finish the Rambler. A blue and gray combination will work very nicely on this project. (See section on "Finishing and Coloring of Projects" in Chap. I.)

DETAILS OF THE RAMBLER

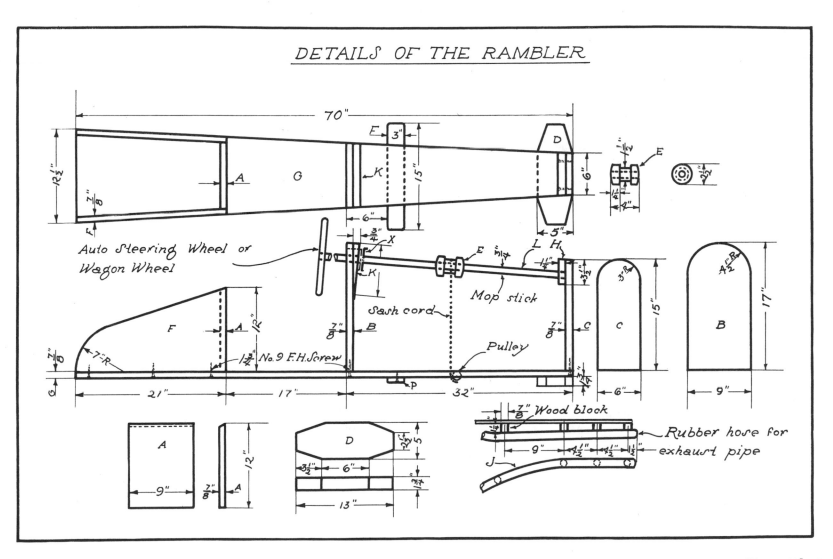

PLATE 24.

[Page 61]

THE SPEEDSTER

The Speedster illustrated in Plates 25 and 26 is another type of pushmobile that a boy can make in his leisure time at home or in the school shop. This little car is very simple and can be made very attractive. A softwood that is light in weight, such as butternut or basswood, is suggested for the framework of the Speedster.

Bill of Material. Finished dimensions.

1 pc.	7/8 x 10	x 55	Baseboard (A)
1 pc.	3/4 x 5 3/4 x 10		Back Piece (B)
1 pc.	3/4 x 10	x 11	Seat Back (C)
1 pc.	3/4 x 10	x 13	Cowl Board (D)
1 pc.	3/4 x 7	x 11 1/2	Radiator Front (E)
2 pc.	3/4 x 10	x 12 1/4	Sides (F)
1 pc.	3/4 x 2 1/2 x 10		Top Piece (R)
1 pc.	3/4 x 9 1/2 x 10		Door or Cover (S)
1 pc.	1 1/2 x 1 3/4 x 8		Top Front Bolster (G)
1 pc.	1 1/2 x 3 1/8 x 15		Front Lower Bolster (H)
1 pc.	1 1/2 x 5 1/4 x 15		Back Bolster (I)
1 pc.	3/4 x 3	x 17	Foot Rest (J)
1 pc.	1/2 x 6	x 10	Wedge Board (M)
1 pc.	3/4 x 5 1/2 x 7		Front Block (N)
2 pc.	3/4 x 1 1/4 x 20		Sides of Handle (O)
1 pc.	3/4 x 1 1/4 x 13		Crosspiece of Handle (P)
1 pc.	1/8 x 1	x 12 1/2	Band-Iron Brace (T)
1 pc.	1/8 x 1	x 9 3/4	Band-Iron Brace (U)
1 pc. 2 1/2 in. diam. x 4			Cylinder (K)
1 pc. 1 in. diam. x 32			Steering Shaft (L)
1 pc. 28 x 36, Black Iron No. 28 Gauge, Hood			

(See drawings and "Assembling" for wheels, hardware, etc.)

Bolsters, Braces, Hood, etc. Follow the details given in Plates 25 and 26 for shaping all parts of the Speedster. A coping saw may be used to cut around the curves on the bolsters G, H, and I, and around the top ends of D and E. With a 1/2-in. gouge, or a gouge the width of the axles, cut grooves into the bottom edges of the bolsters H and I to receive the axles. Bore all the necessary holes in the wooden parts and in the iron braces U and T. A pattern for the hood is given in Plate 26. It is best to lay out the pattern on paper first. On a piece of wrapping paper 28 by 36 in., lay out 1-in. squares as shown in the drawing. Note where the lines of the pattern cross the squares in Plate 26. Transfer this pattern to the chart by locating the same points on the chart.

Steering Device. A 1-in. dowel or a broomstick may be used for the steering shaft L. A large spool may be used for the cylinder K, or a cylinder may be turned on a lathe or made on the bench with a plane and a spokeshave. A sewing-machine wheel, coaster-wagon wheel, or a wooden wheel turned on a lathe may be used for the steering wheel. Either a sash cord or an aerial wire of several strands will make an excellent steering cable.

Wheels. Coaster-wagon wheels, tricycle wheels, or wooden wheels turned on a lathe may be used on this car. Use steel rods for the axles to fit the wheels. (See "Wooden Wheels for Pushmobile," Pl. 33, and section on "Double-Disc Wheels" in Chap. I.)

Assembling. The back piece B, seat C, cowl D, and radiator front E are fastened to the baseboard A with 1 3/4-in. f.h. screws. (See Pl. 24 for putting these parts into their proper places.) The sides F of the back are nailed to B and C with No. 6 finishing nails. Nail the top piece R to the sides F with No. 6 finishing nails also. The cover S can be hinged to part R next. Use a 3/4 by 1 1/2-in. butt hinge. Fasten the back bolster I to the back end of base A with 1 3/4-in. No. 9 f.h. screws. Fasten the top front

THE SPEEDSTER

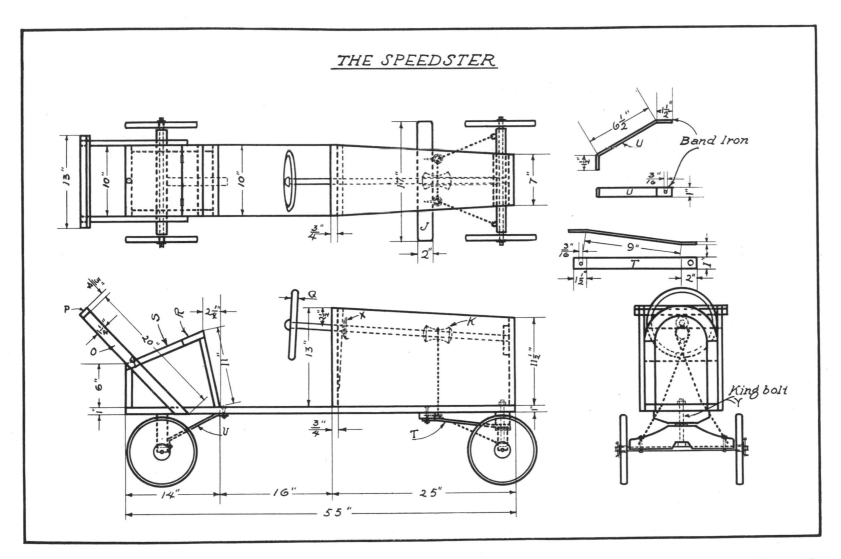

Band Iron

King bolt

PLATE 25.

[Page 63]

bolster G to the front end of baseboard A with 1¾-in. No. 9 f.h. screws also. The rear iron brace U is fastened to base A and to bolster I with 3/16 by 1½- and 2-in. stove bolts. The front end of the iron brace T is held in place by the kingbolt Y, and the other end is attached to A and the foot brace J with a 3/16 by 2-in. stove bolt. Attach the lower front bolster H to G with a ½ by 5½-in. carriage bolt (kingbolt). Use two washers ⅛ by 2 in. in diameter between H and G. The axles are fastened to the back bolster I and the lower front bolster H with 3/16 by 2-in. stove bolts. The wheels are held in place with cotter keys inserted through the ends of each axle. Use washers between the wheels and the bolster, also between the wheels and the cotter keys. Nail the block N to the top part of the radiator front E, and wedge the board M to the top part of cowl D as indicated in Plate 26. At-

tach the steering shaft L next. Nail the cylinder or spool K to the shaft L at the center or at the point shown in the drawing. One end of shaft L fits in the block M. The steering shaft is held in place by a metal washer and a cotter key or nail. The key, or nail, is placed through the shaft at the point X. Wind the steering cable around the spool or cylinder K, carry it through the holes and the screw eyes in base A, and fasten the ends to large screw eyes on each side of the lower bolster H. The black-iron hood can be fastened to the cowl board D, and the radiator board E, with box nails or 1-in. r.h. screws.

Finishing. A simple gloss paint is suggested to color and finish the Speedster. A combination of gray trimmed with black is suggested for this car. (See color chart and section on "Finishing and Coloring of Projects" in Chap. I.)

DETAILS OF THE SPEEDSTER

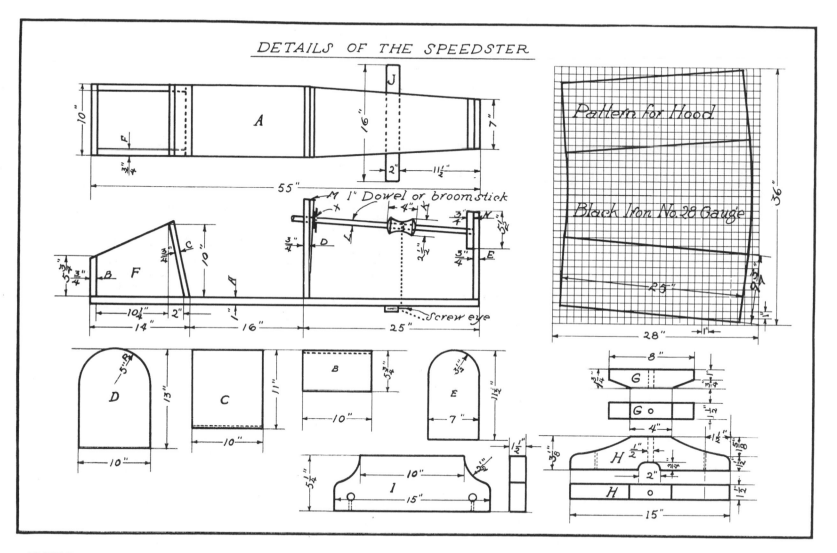

PLATE 26.

[Page 65]

THE RACER

The Racer furnishes another type of pushmobile that the young "speed king" may work on as his next project. Metal is the principal material used in the construction of the Racer. The wooden parts of the Racer, except the front bolster, should be built of softwood such as beechnut, butternut, or pine. The front bolster I should be made of hardwood.

Bill of Material. Finished dimensions.
1 pc. 1 x 13 x 72   Bottom Board (A)
1 pc. ¾ x 13 x 16½   Seat Back (B)
2 pc. ¾ x 8 x 22   Seat Braces (C)
1 pc. ¾ x 10 x 13   Seat (D)
1 pc. 1½ x 5¾ x 10¾   Front Bolster (I)
1 pc. 1½ x 5¼ x 14   Back Bolster (J)
2 pc. ⅞ x 7½ x 18½   Back Fender Braces (S)
2 pc. ⅞ x 8 x 17½   Front Fender Braces (T)
1 Wheel 1 in. thick, 12 in. diam., Steering Wheel (P)

Metal Parts.
1 pc. 1/16 x 1 x 51   Part (E) (Band Iron)
1 pc. 1/16 x 1 x 38   Front (F) (Band Iron)
1 pc. 1/16 x 1 x 20   Shaft Brace (H)
2 pc. ⅛ x ¾ x 1½   Corner Irons (K)
1 pc. 3/16 x ¾ x 13¾   Front Bolster Iron (L)
1 pc. ⅛ x ⅝ x 6¾   Connecting Arm (N)
1 pc. ⅛ x ¾ x 12   Tie Rod (O)
1 pc. ½ in. diam. x 46 Steering Shaft (G)
2 Steering Knuckles (M-1 or M-2)
2 pc. 5 x 30   Black Iron No. 24 Gauge, Back Fenders (Q)
2 pc. 6½ x 25½   Black Iron No. 24 Gauge, Front Fenders (R)
2 pc. 24 x 72¼   Black Iron No. 28 Gauge, Body Parts (U)
1 pc. 13 x 24½   Black Iron No. 28 Gauge, Top of Back (V)
(See drawings and "Assembling" for wheels, hardware, etc.)

Framework. The details given in Plates 28 and 29 show clearly how the different parts of the Racer are made. Such parts as the braces C, bolster I, bolster J, fender braces S and T should be carefully laid out with a pair of dividers. Cut to the curved lines with a coping, turning, jig, or band saw and finish with a spokeshave, chisel, and sandpaper.

FIG. 12. THE RACER.

Metal Parts. Locate and drill all necessary holes in the parts E and F, cross brace H, and other metal parts of the car. The loop in the center of brace H can be shaped around a rod or the steering shaft itself.

Steering Device. The steering device for the Racer may be obtained from a discarded toy automobile or one may be constructed according to the suggested details given in Plate 28. M-1 and M-2 show two ways of making the steering knuckles. In M-2 the knuckles are made from ⅛-in. band iron and a ⅜ by 3-in. machine bolt. The metal will have to be heated so as to bend the steering arm of M-2 to the proper angle and shape.

THE RACER

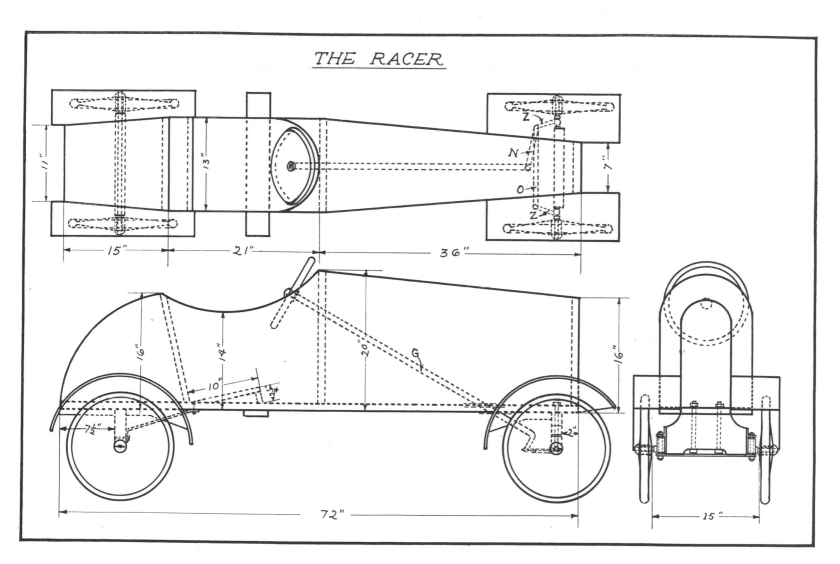

PLATE 27.

[Page 67]

These parts, or other metal parts of the steering device, may be purchased ready-made or they may be made by your local blacksmith. A sewing-machine wheel, coaster-wagon wheel, or a wooden wheel turned on a lathe can be used for the steering wheel.

Wheels. See wheels for the Gopher Special and the section on wheels in Chapter I.

Patterns. Lay out your patterns for the body of the car and fenders according to the directions given for the Gopher-Special patterns, and Plate 29.

Assembling. Fasten the seat back B to the bottom board A with 1¾-in. No. 9 f.h. screws. Nail seat D to block Y and to A. The braces C are fastened to B and to the back part of A with 1½-in. No. 9 f.h. screws. Fasten the band-iron parts E and F to baseboard A with ³⁄₁₆ by 1¼-in. rivets. (See Pl. 28.) Attach the shaft brace H to the sides of part E with ³⁄₁₆ by ½-in. rivets. Fasten the back bolster J to A with 1½-in. No. 9 f.h. screws. Attach the back axle to bolster J with ³⁄₁₆ by 2-in. stove bolts. Attach the front bolster I to the front part A with two ½ by 6½-in. carriage bolts. Fasten the steering-knuckle corner irons K to the ends of bolster I with 1¾-in. No. 9 f.h. screws, and the iron brace L to the lower edge of bolster I with 1¼-in. No. 8 f.h. screws. Use ¼ by 3-in. machine bolts for the two steering-knuckle pivot bolts.

Attach the steering shaft G next. Use a washer on each side of the loop of brace H. The shaft is held in place by means of cotter keys through the shaft on each side of the loop of the brace H. Nail large sheet-metal washers to base A where shaft G passes through A. Connect the two black-iron half patterns U by means of a seam at the top center. Fasten this metal to the parts E and the front piece F of the car with ¼-in. rivets. The rivets may be forced through the metal by placing the rivets into the holes in the band iron first, and then they may be riveted on the outside of the sheet metal. Nail the metal to the edge of base A and braces C with box nails. In like manner, nail the top piece V to the edges of braces C. Fasten the tie rod O to the steering knuckles Z with ¼ by ½-in. bolts. One end of the connecting arm N is connected with a ¼ by ½-in. bolt to the tie rod at one of the steering knuckles and the other end is attached to the steering shaft with a cotter key. Fasten the fender braces S and T to the edges of base A with 1½-in. No. 9 f.h. screws. Nail the fender to the top edges of these braces with box nails. (See Plates 27 and 29.) The wheels may be held in place by means of cotter keys and caps.

Finishing. Follow the directions given for finishing the Gopher Special.

DETAILS OF THE RACER

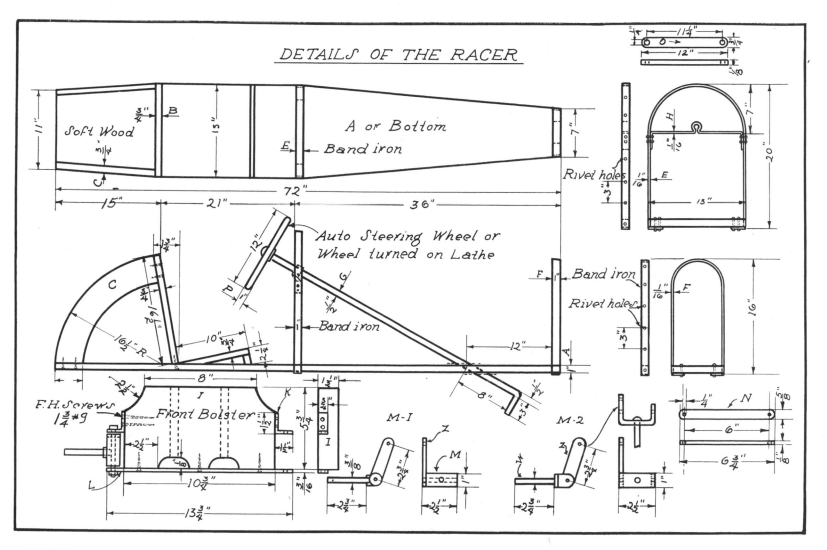

Soft Wood

A or Bottom
Band iron

Auto Steering Wheel or
Wheel turned on Lathe

Band iron

Band iron

Rivet holes

Front Bolster

F.H.Screws
1¾ #9

M-1   M-2

Rivet holes

PLATE 28.

[Page 69]

DETAILS AND PATTERNS OF THE RACER

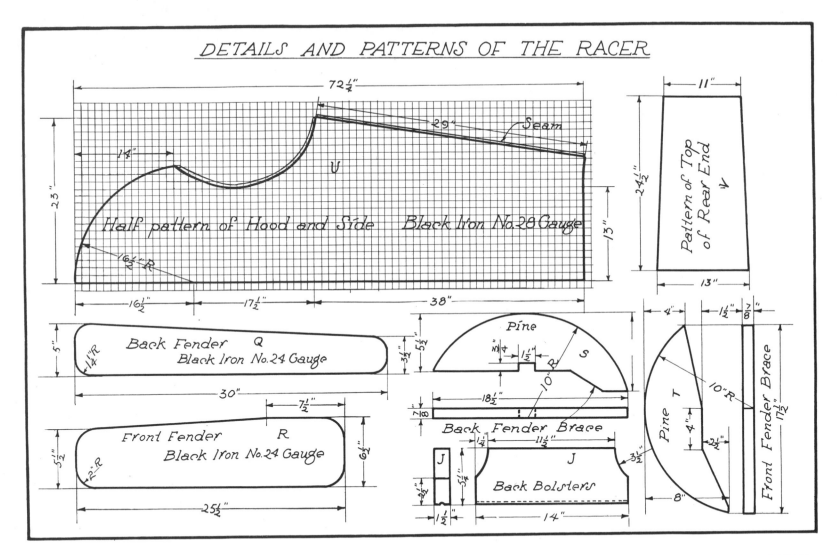

72¼"

29" Seam

14"

23"

U

Half pattern of Hood and Side   Black Iron No.28 Gauge

13"

16½"R

16½"   17½"   38"

Pattern of Top
of Rear End
V

11"

24½"

13"

5"   Back Fender   Q
    Black Iron No.24 Gauge   3½"   5½"

1¼"R

30"   7½"

Front Fender   R
    Black Iron No.24 Gauge   6½"

5½"

2"R   25½"

Pine
¾"   1½"   S   R
18½"   10"R
⅞"   Back Fender Brace
1¼"   11½"   J
J   3½"
Back Bolsters
2½"   5¾"
1½"   14"

4"   1½"   ⅞"

10"R   Front Fender Brace

Pine   T   4"
2½"
8"   17½"

PLATE 29.

THE GOPHER SPECIAL

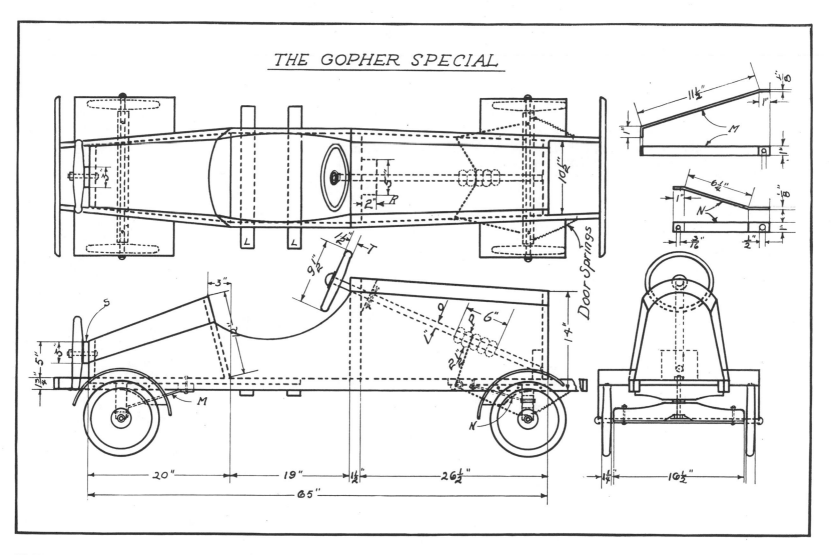

PLATE 30.

[Page 71]

In the Gopher Special we have an up-to-date racing car of the type most suitable for a boy. It is sturdily designed and can be made very attractive. A boy may use his own ingenuity in adding accessories to his car such as headlights, motometer, windshield, etc. The framework of the Gopher Special may be constructed of softwood such as pine or butternut, except the two sides A. The sides A should be made of birch, oak, or some other suitable hardwood.

Bill of Material. Finished dimensions.

2 pc. ¾ x 1¾ x 77 Side Pieces (A) (Hardwood)
2 pc. ¾ x 1½ x 13¼ Sides of Cowl (B) (Hardwood)
1 pc. 1½ x 5¾ x 10½ Top of Cowl (B) (Softwood)
1 pc. ¾ x 12 x 12¼ Radiator Front (C)
1 pc. ¾ x 12 x 14½ Seat Back (D)
1 pc. ¾ x 5 x 10½ Back Piece (E)
1 pc. ¾ x 13 x 29 Back Bottom Board (F)
1 pc. ¾ x 12 x 14 Front Bottom Board (G)
1 pc. 1½ x 2¼ x 12¼ Top Front Bolster (H)
1 pc. 1½ x 2½ x 19 Lower Front Bolster (I)
1 pc. 1½ x 5 x 19 Back Bolster (J)
2 pc. ¾ x 1¾ x 22½ Bumpers (K)
2 pc. ¾ x 2 x 21 Running Boards (L)
1 pc. ⅛ x 1 x 13¾ Brace (M) (Band Iron)
1 pc. ⅛ x 1 x 9⅜ Brace (N) (Band Iron)
1 pc. 1½ x 4 x 5 Front Guide Block (Q)
1 pc. 2 x 5 x 5½ Cowl Block (R)
1 pc. 1 x 3 x 3 Spare-Wheel Block (S)
4 pc. ¾ x 5 x 12 Fender Braces (U) (See Pl. 30)
1 Wheel, 1½ in. thick, 9½ in. diam., Steering Wheel (T)
1 pc. 1 in. diam. x 33 Steering Shaft (O)
1 pc. 2½ in. diam. x 6 Cylinder (P)
1 pc. 29 x 40 Black Iron No. 28 Gauge, Hood (V)
1 pc. 22 x 34 Black Iron No. 28 Gauge, Back (W)
2 pc. 22½ x 13 Black Iron No. 28 Gauge, Sides (X)
2 pc. 5½ x 23 Black Iron No. 24 Gauge, Front Fenders (Z)
2 pc. 6½ x 22 Black Iron No. 24 Gauge, Back Fenders (Y)
(See drawings and "Assembling" for wheels, hardware, etc.)

Framework. The details given in Plates 30, 31, and 32 show clearly how the different parts of the Gopher Special are made and assembled. Such pieces as B, C, D, and E should be carefully laid out with a pair of dividers. Special attention should be given to the cowl part B. Cut to the curved lines with a coping, turning, or band saw, and finish with a spokeshave, plane, and sandpaper. The curves in bolsters H, I, and J should be treated in like manner. With a gouge the width of the axles, cut grooves

FIG. 13. THE GOPHER SPECIAL.

into the lower edges of the bolsters I and J to receive the axles. Bore all necessary holes in the wooden parts, and in the iron braces and the axles.

Steering Device. Use a mopstick or a broomstick for the steering shaft O. The cylinder P may be turned on a lathe, or a block may be easily shaped on the bench. A sewing-machine wheel, a coaster-wagon wheel, or a wooden wheel turned on a

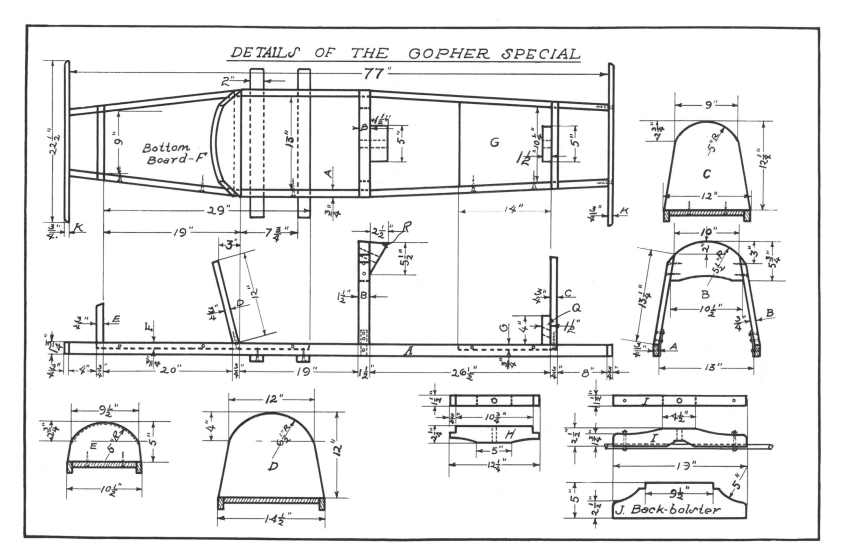

DETAILS OF THE GOPHER SPECIAL

PLATE 31.

[Page 73]

lathe may be used for the steering wheel. If a lathe is available, make the wheel as shown in Plate 30. Either a piece of sash cord or aerial wire of several strands will make an excellent steering cable. Small pulleys or window-sash pulleys work very well for cable guides.

Wheels. Coaster-wagon wheels, or wooden wheels turned on a lathe, may be used on this car. Use steel rods to fit the wheels for the axles. (See Pl. 33, and sections on "Wooden Wheels," and "Double-Disc Wheels" in Chap. I.)

Patterns. Patterns of the hood, back, sides, and fenders for the Gopher Special have been worked out in Plate 32. It is best to lay out the patterns on paper first. On sheets of heavy wrapping paper of the required size, lay out 1-in. squares as shown in Plate 32. Notice where the lines of the patterns cross each square in the drawing. Transfer these patterns to the charts of squares by locating the same points on the charts. Connect all the points with the lines free-hand. The paper patterns can be traced on the metal next.

Assembling. The two side pieces A are fastened to the bottom of the boards F and G with 1¾-in. No. 9 f.h. screws. Fasten parts D, C, and E to the bottom boards F and G with 1¾-in. No. 9 f.h. screws also. The cowl part B is fastened to the sides A with $\frac{1}{16}$ by 1 by 4-in. irons and screws. (See Pl. 31 to get the parts in their proper places.) Fasten the back bolster J to the back end of F with 1¾-in. No. 9 f.h. screws. In like manner, fasten the front top bolster H to the front of the bottom part G. The rear iron brace M is fastened to the board F with a $\frac{3}{16}$ by 1-in. stove bolt and to the rear bolster J with a $\frac{3}{16}$ by 2-in. stove bolt.

The front end of the iron brace N is held in place by the kingbolt and the other end is attached to board G with a $\frac{3}{16}$ by 1-in. stove bolt. Attach the lower front bolster I to H and to the front part of the car with a ½ by 5½-in. carriage bolt (kingbolt). Use two large washers between H and I. The axles are fastened to the back bolster J and the lower front bolster H with $\frac{3}{16}$ by 2-in. stove bolts. The wheels are held in place with cotter keys or caps. Use washers between the wheels and bolsters, also between the wheels and cotter keys or caps.

Nail the block Q to the bottom part of the radiator front C, and wedge the block R to the top part of the cowl B as indicated in Plate 31. Bore 1-in. holes through these pieces to receive the steering shaft. Attach the steering shaft O next. Nail the cylinder or spool P to the shaft O at the point indicated in Plate 30. One end of the shaft O fits and turns in the block Q. The steering shaft is held in place by a metal washer placed against R, and by a cotter key or nail. Wind the steering cable around the spool P; carry it through the pulleys which are attached to the sides of A, and fasten the ends to screw eyes on each side of the lower bolster I.

The steering wheel may be fastened to the shaft by means of a pin or r.h. screw through the hub of wheel and shaft. The metal hood V, the back W, and the sides X are attached to the framework of the car with shingle nails or box nails. Use 1-in. No. 7 r.h. screws or shingle nails to fasten the fenders Y and Z to the top edges of the fender braces.

Finishing. An automobile enamel of a desirable color is suggested to color and finish the Gopher Special. There are many beautiful auto enamels on the market. An outside gloss paint may also be used on this project. (See section on "Finishing and Coloring of Projects" in Chap. I.)

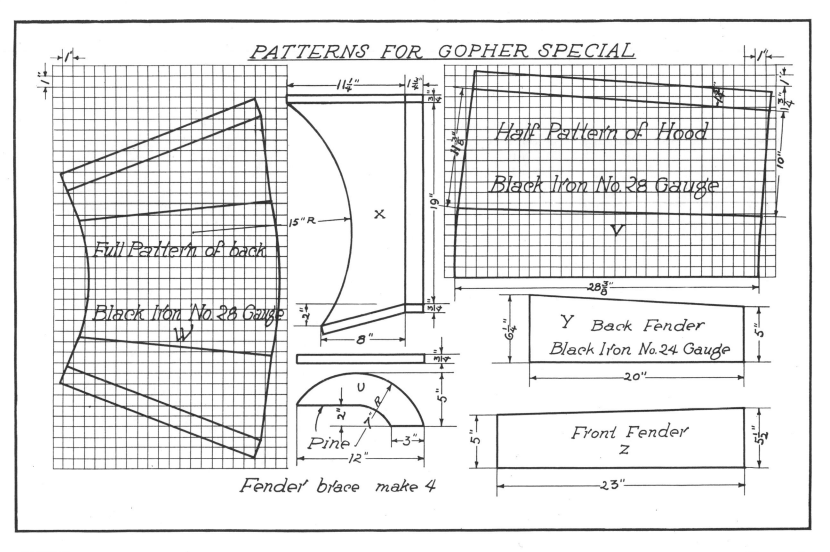

PATTERNS FOR GOPHER SPECIAL

Half Pattern of Hood

Black Iron No. 28 Gauge

V

Full Pattern of back

Black Iron No. 28 Gauge

W

15" R

X

Y Back Fender

Black Iron No. 24 Gauge

U

Pine

Fender brace make 4

Front Fender

Z

PLATE 32.

[Page 75]

THE SPEED TRUCK

The young "speed king" may use his Speed Truck for either transportation or joy-riding purposes. The combination of materials and processes involved makes the construction of this project very interesting and fascinating to the boy builder, and, at the same time, there is nothing especially difficult about the construction. With the exception of the back axle or eccentric F, the bending and shaping of all metal parts can be done cold. All wooden parts of the Speed Truck, with the exception of the sides A and the connecting rods H, should be made of a softwood, such as butternut, pine, or basswood. Use birch, oak, or ash for the sides A and the connecting rods H.

Bill of Material. Finished dimensions.

```
1 pc.  5/8 x 14½ x 27¾   Bottom (A-A)
2 pc.  3/4 x 4   x 65    Sides (A)
2 pc.  3/4 x 1½ x 14     Sides of (B)
1 pc.  1½ x 6   x 10½    Top Piece of (B)
1 pc.  3/4 x 12  x 16    Radiator Front (C)
1 pc.  3/4 x 13  x 14½   Seat Back (D)
1 pc.  3/4 x 4   x 14½   Back Piece (E)
2 pc.  3/4 x  7/8 x 33½  Connecting Rods (H)
2 pc.  3/4 x 2½ x 8½     Foot Pedals (K)
1 pc.  1½ x 4½ x 11⅛     Top Bolster (M)
1 pc.  1½ x 3⅛ x 17      Lower Bolster (N)
1 pc.  1½ x 2   x 14     Crossbar (W)
1 pc.  3/4 x 2½ x 11     Steering Support (O)
1 pc.  3/4 x 2¼ x 9¼     Steering Support (P)
1 pc.  5/8 x 2   x 20    Bumper (Q)
1 pc.  3/4 x 8½ x 14½    Seat Board (R)
1 pc.  1 in. diam. x 20  Steering Shaft (S)
1 Wheel, 7/8 in. thick, 9 in. diam., Steering Wheel (L)
1 Wheel, 1¼ x 3½         Guide Wheel (T)
```

Metal Parts.
```
1 pc.  ½ in. diam. x 34  Back Axle (F)
2 pc.  1/8 x 1   x 18    Axle Braces (G)
1 pc.  1/8 x 1   x 20½   Back-Axle Brace (X)
2 pc.  1/8 x 3/4 x 9     Connecting Parts (I) (Band Iron)
8 pc.  1/16 x 3/4 x 3    Band Irons (J)
1 pc.  20 x 47 Black Iron No. 28 Gauge
```
(See drawings and "Assembling" for hardware, etc.)

Framework. Parts B and C should be carefully laid out with a pair of dividers. Follow details in Plate 34 closely to make the cowl B. Cut to the curved lines with a coping, turning, or band saw and finish with a spokeshave, plane, and sandpaper. With a gouge the width of the front axle, cut a groove into lower edge of the bolster N to receive the axle.

Metal Parts. The back axle, or eccentric, can best be bent to the shape shown in Plate 34 when it is heated in a forge. The braces G and the connecting irons I can be easily bent cold. The loop part of the irons can be bent around the axle itself or around an iron rod.

Steering Device. Use a broomstick or a 1-in. dowel rod for the steering shaft O. The guide wheel T may be turned on a lathe or cut at the bench with a coping saw or a jig saw. A coaster-wagon wheel or a wheel turned on a lathe may be used for the steering wheel. A piece of sash cord or several strands of aerial wire will make an excellent cable.

Wheels. Wheels for this truck may be turned on a lathe as illustrated in Plate 33. It is best to make them of hardwood. Use a piece of 1½-in. iron pipe for the bushings of the wheels. Great care should be taken in boring a hole at the exact center of each wheel. (See "Boring Devices" in Pl. 1.) The size of the

SPEED TRUCK

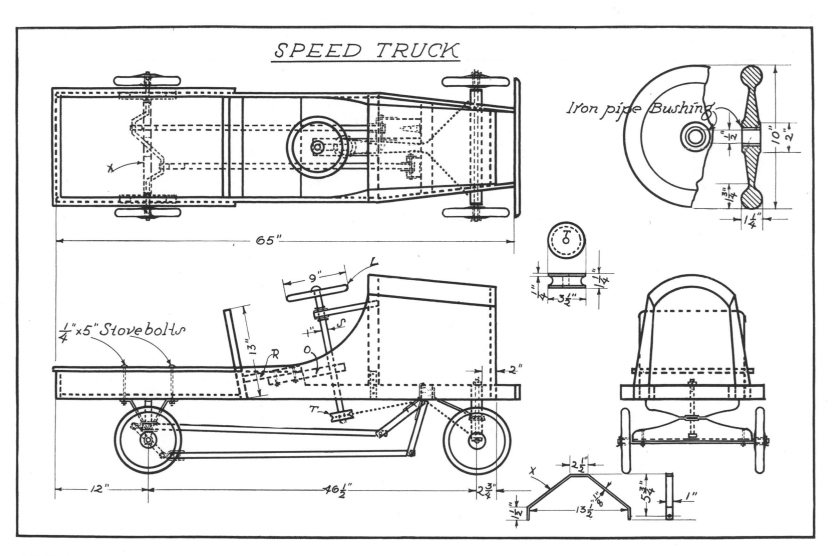

Iron pipe Bushing

¼"x5" Stovebolts

PLATE 33.

[Page 77]

hole should be equal to the outside diameter of the bushing. Force the bushing into the hole of the wheel with a mallet. Bore a ⅛-in. hole diagonally through the hubs and the bushings of the back wheels as shown in Plate 33. The back wheels, bushings, and axle are held together with a ⅛-in. rivet or pin through the hole just bored. The front-wheel bushings should be held in place with steel keys as illustrated in Plate 11.

Pattern for Hood. Follow Plate 33 and directions given for the Gopher-Special pattern to make the hood of the Speed Truck.

Assembling. The two sides A are fastened to the bottom A-A and to parts C, D, E, R, W, and to the top bolster M with 1½-in. No. 9 f.h. screws. (See Pl. 34.) The sides A will bend better if they are steamed or kept in hot water for a short time. The cowl part B is fastened to the sides of A with $\frac{1}{16}$ by 1 by 4-in. iron braces and $\frac{3}{16}$ by 1-in. f.h. stove bolts. Fasten the back axle brace X to bottom board A-A with $\frac{3}{16}$ by 1-in. f.h. stove bolts. Attach the steering-shaft support P to the lower part of the block of section B with 1¾-in. No. 9 f.h. screws and iron braces. Fasten the shaft support O to seat R with $\frac{3}{16}$ by 2-in. f.h. stove bolts. Fasten the connecting irons I around axle F and the connecting rods H with $\frac{3}{16}$ by 1¼-in. rivets.

Fasten the two irons J to the front ends of the connecting rods with $\frac{3}{16}$ by 1¼-in. rivets, and the two irons J to one end of K with 1-in. No. 8 f.h. screws. Connect pedals K and the connecting rods with ¼ by 3½-in. machine bolts. Attach the braces G, with rear axle in place, to the lower edge of sides A with ¼ by 5-in. stove bolts. Countersink the heads in the wood. Attach one end of the pedals K to crossbar W with T or strap hinges. Fasten the lower front bolster N to M with a ½ by 8-in. carriage bolt (kingbolt). Use two ⅛ by 2-in. washers between M and N. The front axle is fastened to the lower front bolster N with $\frac{3}{16}$ by 2-in. stove bolts. The back wheels are held to the back axle or eccentric with ⅛ by 3-in. pins through the hubs of wheels, bushings, and axle. The front wheels are held in place with cotter keys. Attach the steering shaft S to the car next. Nail the guide wheel T to one end of the steering shaft S. The shaft S is held in place by metal washers and a cotter key through the shaft on each side of the support O. Fasten the steering wheel to the top end of shaft S with a 1¼-in. No. 8 r.h. screw. Wind the steering cable around guide wheel T, and carry it through the pulleys which are attached to the center of the crossbar W, then fasten the ends of the cable to the screw eyes at each side of the lower bolster N. The metal hood cover and the side pieces are fastened to the framework of the car with shingle nails or box nails.

Finishing. Follow the directions given for finishing the Gopher Special, page 74.

DOLL COACH

The Doll Coach illustrated in Plates 35 and 36 represents an up-to-date carriage for a child's dolly or doll family. This project can be worked out as a very fine Christmas or birthday gift. It can be made very substantial and attractive. There is nothing difficult about the project and it is well within the abilities of 8A and 9B students. With the exception of the wheels and axles, the Doll Coach may be constructed of softwood such as butternut, beechnut, white pine, or poplar. It is best to make the wheels and axles of hardwood.

Bill of Material. Finished dimensions.
2 pc. ½ x 10¼ x 15⅞ Sides and Doors (A-A)
1 pc. ½ x 9¼ x 10¼ Front (B)
1 pc. ½ x 5⅜ x 10⅛ Cowl Support (C)

DETAILS OF THE SPEED TRUCK

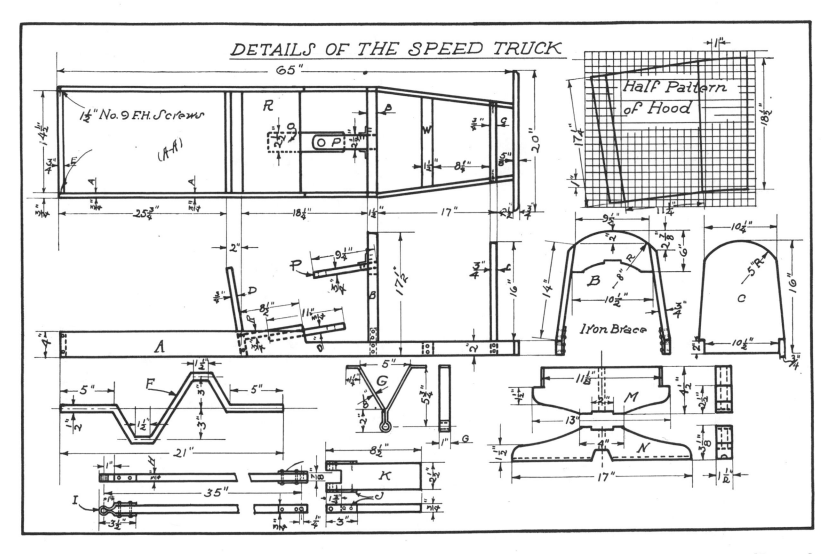

Half Pattern of Hood

PLATE 34.

[Page 79]

1 pc.   ¾ x 10¼ x 9¾ Back (D)
1 pc.   ¾ x 5¾ x 5¼ Radiator Front (E)
1 pc.   ⅝ x 11¼ x 16¼ Top (F)
1 pc.   ½ x 10¼ x 25½ Bottom (G)
2 pc.   ¾ x ⅞ x 11⅝ Axles (I)
2 pc.   ⅜ x ½ x 14½ Bumpers (J)
2 pc.   ½ x ½ x 2⅜ Front-Bumper Braces (K)
2 pc.   ½ x ½ x 6¼ Back-Bumper Braces (L)
2 pc.   ⅜ x 2 x 14 Running Board (M)
2 pc.   ⅜ x 1 x 14 Running Board Brace (N)
4 pc.   5⁄16 x 3⅛ x 6⅛ Fender Supports (O)
1 pc.   13½ x 20   Black Iron No. 28 Gauge, Hood (P)
2 pc.   1⅞ x 13¾   Black Iron No. 28 Gauge, Rear Fenders (Q)
2 pc.   2⅜ x 11¼   Black Iron No. 28 Gauge, Front Fenders (R)
1 pc.   ⅜ in. diam. x 64 Handle (S) (Iron Rod)
2 pc.   ⅞ in. diam. x 4 Handle Braces (T)
5 Wheels, 1¼ in. thick, 5½ in. diam. (H)
(See drawings and "Assembling" for hardware, windshield, etc.)

Sides. Follow the details in Plate 36 to get the shape of each part. Make each side A, including the door A¹, out of one piece of stock. After these parts are properly shaped, cut the doors off with a fine crosscut saw. Locate all windows or openings. Bore a ¼-in. hole at one corner of each of these spaces and then use a coping saw to cut out the openings for the windows.

Wheels. The wheels should be turned on a lathe showing the balloon-tire effect. However, if a lathe is not available, neat wheels may be cut with the use of a coping saw, jig saw, or turning saw. (See wheels in Plates 35 and 11; also section on "Wooden Wheels" in Chap. I.)

Hood. Lay out the pattern of the hood on paper first. On a piece of drawing paper 14 by 20 in. lay out 1-in. squares as shown in Plate 36. Note where the lines of the pattern cross each square in the drawing. Transfer this pattern to the chart of squares. Connect all points with a line free-hand. The paper pattern is then ready to be traced on the metal.

Handle. Make the handle of ⅜-in. soft-iron rod. Drill two 3⁄16-in. holes near each end of the rod. Bend the iron to the shape

indicated in Plate 35 and Figure 14. The radius of the bend must be sufficient to allow foot clearance for the child who pushes.

Assembling. The body of the coach is assembled with glue and 1½-in. brads. Such parts of the coach as the top, back, and sides are rounded off to the desired shape after the body has been assembled. This can be done with a plane, spokeshave, file and sandpaper.

FIG. 14. DOLL COACH.

The axles I are fastened to bottom G of the car with 3⁄16 by 1½-in. stove bolts. Fasten the front-bumper braces K to bottom board G with ⅞-in. No. 7 f.h. screws. (See Pl. 35.) The back-bumper braces L may be fastened to the car with 1¼-in. No. 8 f.h. screws. Fasten bumpers to the braces with 1½-in. No. 8 r.h. screws.

Nail the running board M to support N. Attach these pieces to the sides of the car with 1½-in. brads, or 1¼-in. screws. Nail

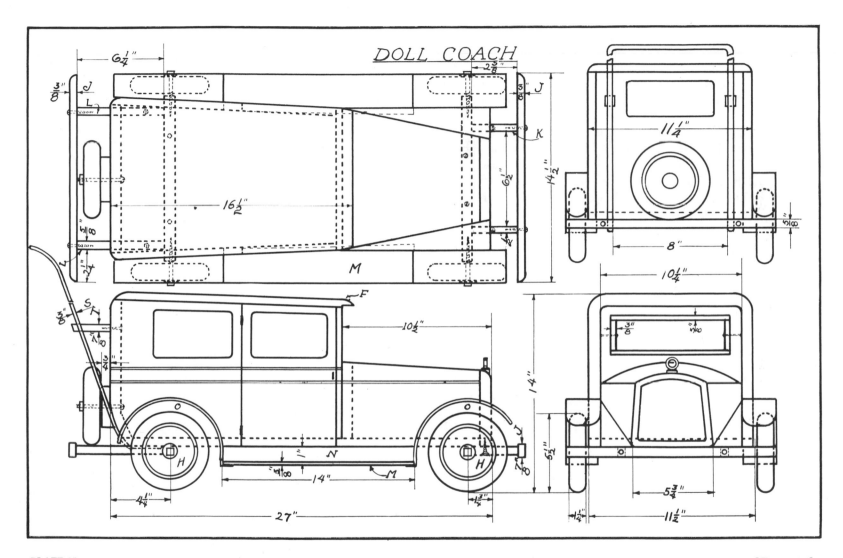

DOLL COACH

PLATE 35.

[Page 81]

front-fender supports O to the front of bottom G, and the back-fender supports to the body of the car. The fenders are fastened to the top edges of these pieces and to the running board with $\frac{1}{2}$-in. escutcheon pins or box nails. (See Plates 35 and 36.) Fasten the metal hood P to C and E with $\frac{1}{2}$-in. escutcheon pins also.

The wheels are fastened to the axles with $\frac{1}{4}$ by 3-in. lag screws. The spare wheel is attached to the block and the back of the car with a $\frac{3}{16}$ by 2-in. stove bolt. The handle braces T are attached to the back end D with $1\frac{1}{2}$-in. No. 9 f.h. screws. Run the iron handle S through $\frac{3}{8}$-in. holes at the ends of the braces T and attach the lower ends to the bottom of the car with $\frac{3}{16}$ by $1\frac{1}{2}$-in. stove bolts. A boy may use his own initiative and ingenuity in adding more accessories to this car such as a windshield, steering wheel, seats, etc.

Finishing. A gloss paint or an automobile enamel may be used to color and finish the Doll Coach. Paint or enamel the top, fenders, and running boards black. Paint the lower part of the car a nice blue and the upper part gray or some similar color. A boy may get his color scheme from some of the beautiful colors of our modern automobiles. (See section on "Finishing and Coloring of Projects" in Chap. I.)

DETAILS DOLL COACH

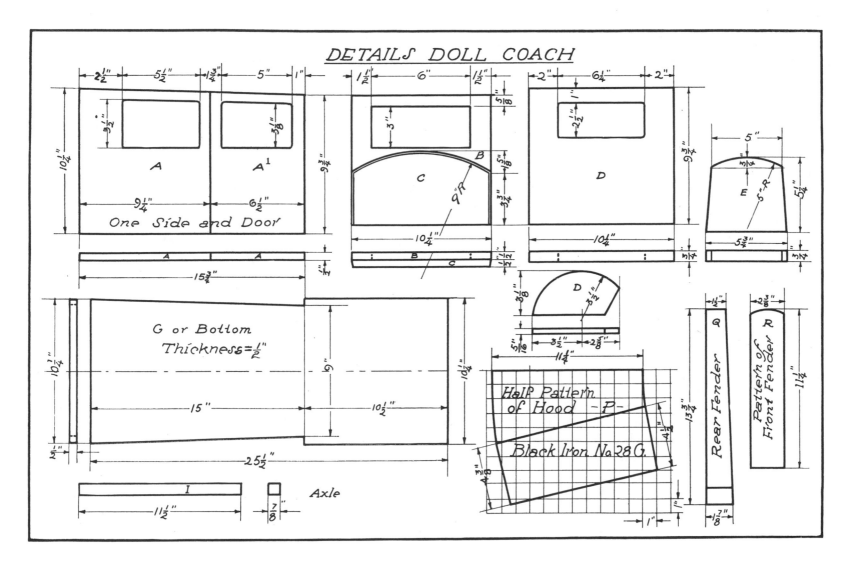

PLATE 36.

[Page 83]

CHAPTER V
WINTER PROJECTS

SLED

THE well-constructed homemade sled is always a source of great pride to its owner. The sled shown in Plate 37 can be made very simple, light, durable, and strong. Use a softwood to make this sled. Butternut or beechnut are very light in weight and are especially recommended.

Bill of Material. Finished dimensions.
2 pc. ¾ x 4¼ x 39   Runners (A)
1 pc. ⅝ x 11   x 22½ Top (B)
3 pc. ¾ x 1⅜ x 12   Braces (C)
6 pc. ¼ x 1½ Corner Irons (G)
1 pc. ¾ in. diam. x 12½ Dowel (D)
6 pc. ⅜ in. diam. x 3⅝ Birch Dowels (E)
2 pc. half-round ¾ x 46 Iron Shoes (F)

Runners. Three patterns for runners are given in Plate 37. Lay out the runners according to one of these designs. In runner A, the front end has been marked out into squares. These squares will help in laying out a nice curve. Note where the curves intersect the lines in each square on the pattern. (Pl. 37.) Locate these same points on the runner and connect the points by a line. Runners X and Y may be laid out with a pair of dividers or compasses as shown in Plate 37. Make the mortises in the runners ½ in. deep and 1 in. wide. Cut these with a ⅜-in. mortising or framing chisel. The runners should be reinforced with ⅜-in. hardwood dowels. Bore a ⅜-in. hole the full width of the runner. Put hot glue into the hole and on the dowel, and drive the dowel into the hole.

Assembling. Fasten the braces C to the runners first. Use glue on the mortise-and-tenon joints. Attach the corner iron to braces C and runners A with ¾-in. No. 8 f.h. screws. These irons will help to make the sled solid and strong. Fasten the top B to the braces C with 1¼-in. No. 8 f.h. screws. Attach the half-round iron shoes to the runners with 1-in. No. 8 f.h. screws. Bend the shoes on the runners. The holes in the bottom of the shoes should be countersunk. Half-round iron or band iron suitable for sled shoes may be obtained from either a blacksmith shop or an iron store. Bore ¾-in. holes at the front end of the runners to receive the rod D. These holes should be bored after the iron shoes have been attached. The iron around these ends will prevent the wood from splitting.

Finishing. Use an outside gloss paint or stain to finish this project. Paint the runners A a bright red, and the top B and edges a bright yellow. (See section on "Finishing and Coloring of Projects" in Chap. I.)

SLED

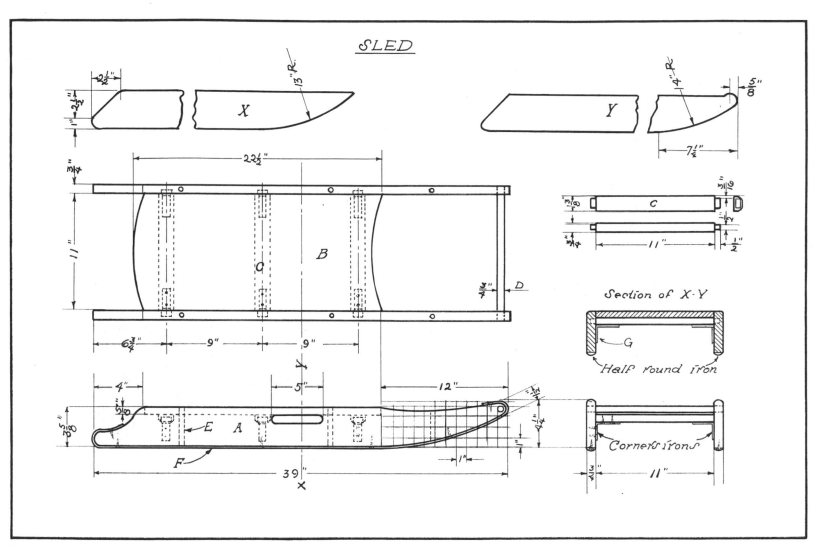

PLATE 37.

[Page 85]

BOBSLED

A boy living in a section of the country where there is snow a greater part of the winter considers his Bobsled the pride of his possessions. The Bobsled in Plates 38 and 39 is not difficult to construct and involves a combination of materials well adapted to the general shop in the school. Hardwood, such as birch or oak should be used for all the wooden parts of the Bobsled, except the box B. The box should be made of a light softwood, such as butternut, pine, or beechnut, or any other light softwood available.

Bill of Material. Finished dimensions.

2 pc. ⅝ x 5 x 52 Sides of Box (B)
2 pc. ⅝ x 5 x 16½ Ends of (B)
1 pc. ⅝ x 17¾ x 52 Bottom of (B)
1 pc. ½ x 2 x 18¼ Front Piece of Frame (B)
1 pc. ½ x 1 x 18¼ Back Piece of Frame (B)
2 pc. ½ x 1 x 50 Side Pieces of Frame of (B)
4 pc. 1 x 5 x 25 Runners (A)
1 pc. 1½ x 2 x 21¾ Top Back Bolster (C)
2 pc. 2 x 2 x 21¾ Lower Back and Front Bolster (D)
1 pc. 1½ x 2 x 21¾ Top Front Bolster (E)
2 pc. 1 x 1½ x 15½ Runner Guides (F)
1 pc. ¾ x 1½ x 16½ Back Tongue (G)
1 pc. ¾ x 2½ x 46 Tongue (H)
2 pc. ¾ x 1½ x 21½ Back and Front Cross Pieces (P)
2 pc. ¾ x 2 x 22 Box Guides (Q)
4 pc. 1⁄16 x ¾ x 14¼ Runner Braces (I) (Band Iron)
4 pc. 1⁄16 or 3⁄32 x 1 x 34 Shoes (J) (Band Iron)
4 pc. 1⁄16 x ¾ x 8 Tongue Braces (K) (Band Iron)
2 pc. 1⁄16 x ¾ x 4½ Back Tongue Iron (N)
1 pc. 1⁄16 x ½ x 7 Hook (O) (Band Iron)
8 pc. ¾ in. diam. x 4 Dowels (L) and (M)

(See Pl. 38 and "Assembling" for hardware, etc.)

Runners, Bolsters, etc. The details given in Plates 38 and 39 show clearly how the different parts of the Bobsled are made and assembled. The front end of runner A has been marked out into squares. These squares will help in laying out a nice curve. Draw similar squares on one of the runners making the squares 1 in. each way. Notice where the curves intersect the lines in each

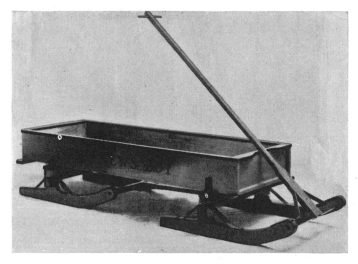

FIG. 15. BOBSLED.

square on the runner pattern, Plate 39. Locate the same points on the runner and connect the points with a line forming the desired curve. Such parts as the bolsters C, D, E, guide pieces Q, and the tongue H should be laid out carefully with a pair of dividers. Cut to curved lines with a coping, turning, or band

BOB SLED

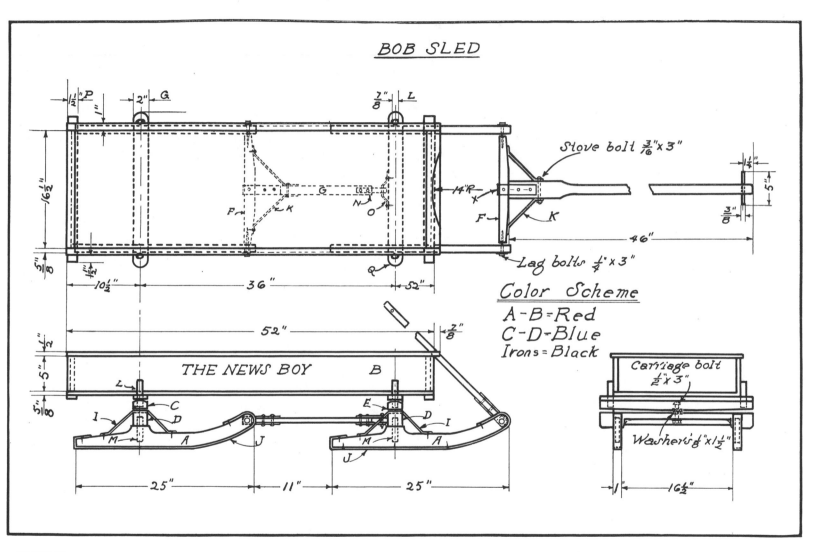

Stove bolt $\frac{3}{16}$" x 3"

Lag bolts $\frac{1}{4}$" x 3"

Color Scheme
A - B = Red
C - D = Blue
Irons = Black

THE NEWS BOY

Carriage bolt $\frac{1}{2}$" x 3"

Washers $\frac{3}{8}$" x $1\frac{1}{2}$"

PLATE 38.

[Page 87]

saw, and finish with spokeshave, file, plane, and sandpaper. Make the top part of C and E round. Bore all necessary holes in the wooden parts.

Band-Iron Parts. Locate and drill all necessary holes in these iron parts before doing any bending. Countersink the holes in the iron shoes. Any of the band-iron parts used in the Bobsled can be easily bent cold. (See sections on "Band Iron" and "Drilling in Iron" in Chap. I.)

Assembling. Bend the band-iron shoes to the shape of the runners and fasten these to the runners with $\frac{3}{4}$-in. No. 7 f.h. screws. Fasten the lower back bolster D to the back runners with $\frac{3}{4}$ by $3\frac{1}{2}$-in. dowels, and iron braces I. The iron braces I are fastened at the tops of bolsters with two $\frac{3}{4}$-in. No. 8 f.h. screws and to the runners with $\frac{3}{4}$-in. No. 8 r.h. screws. In like manner, the lower front bolster D is fastened to the front runners. Attach the tongue H to front runner guide F with braces K and a piece of sheet metal X as shown in Plate 38. The braces K are attached to F and H with 1-in. No. 9 r.h. screws and a $\frac{3}{16}$ by 3-in. stove bolt. The metal piece X is fastened to F and H with $\frac{3}{16}$ by 1-in. stove bolts. In a similar manner, the back tongue G is fastened to the back-runner guide K. Fasten the iron N to the end of tongue G with two $\frac{3}{16}$ by 2-in. stove bolts.

Fasten the back and front guides F to the runners with $\frac{1}{4}$ by 3-in. lag screws. Use washers between the heads of the screws and the runners. Attach the top back bolster C to bolster D with two $\frac{3}{16}$ by $2\frac{1}{2}$-in. stove bolts. The front top bolster E is fastened to lower bolster D with a $\frac{1}{2}$ by 3-in. carriage bolt (kingbolt). Use two large washers between E and D. Fasten the iron hook O to the front piece D at the center point to receive the irons N of G.

The box B may be assembled with glue and 2-in. finishing nails. Fasten end crosspieces P and the guide Q to the bottom of box B with $1\frac{1}{4}$-in. No. 8 f.h. screws. The holes at the ends of each guide Q should be larger than the dowels L and should be oblong in shape. Allow enough play at these points to enable the box to pivot freely on the round parts of the top bolsters C and E.

Finishing. A gloss paint, stain, or enamel may be used to color and finish the Bobsled. (See section on "Finishing and Coloring of Projects" in Chap. I.) A color scheme shown in Plate 38 is suggested for **this project.**

DETAILS OF BOB SLED

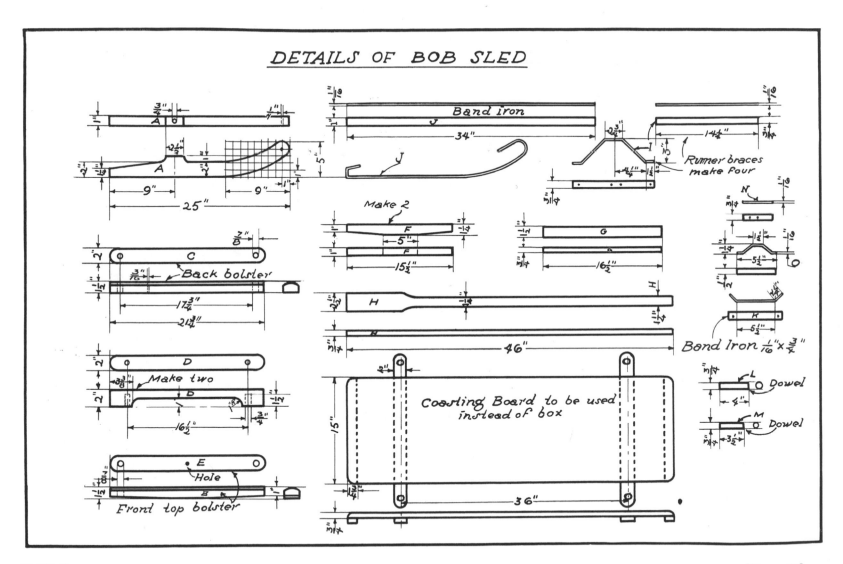

PLATE 39.

[Page 89]

Coasting is probably the best sport for boys during the winter wherever there are coasting facilities. Coasting on a Scootersled is a lot of fun, and it is a sport that every boy and girl will take part in during their leisure time. The Scootersled shown in Plate 40 should be constructed of hardwood such as hickory, birch, or ash.

Bill of Material. Finished dimensions.
4 pc. ½ x 2½ x 39 Runners (A)
3 pc. ½ x 1½ x 10 Crosspieces (B)
1 pc. ¾ x 1¼ x 28 Tongue (C)
1 pc. 1 x 1½ x 10 Front Piece (G)
2 pc. ⅛ x ¾ x 2 Band Irons (E)
2 pc. ⅛ x ¾ x 3 Corner Irons (F)
1 pc. ⅜ in. diam. x 4½ Dowel Handle (D)

Plane one end of each runner A down to ⅜ in. or ⅚₆ in. thick as shown in the drawing. This can be done easily with a jack plane or a smooth plane. The groove in the front piece G can be cut with a saw or a chisel, or two pieces ½ in. thick may be used instead of one. Bore all necessary holes in the wooden parts and the band-iron parts before assembling the Scootersled. The bending of the runners may be done separately or after the Scootersled has been assembled. (See Pl. 42 for method of bending.)

Assembling. Fasten the three crosspieces to the runners with ¾-in. No. 8 f.h. screws. The front piece is attached to the front ends of runners A with ³⁄₁₆ by 1½-in. stove bolts. The two iron

FIG. 16. SCOOTERSLED.

corner braces F are fastened to front piece G with ³⁄₁₆ by 1½-in. stove bolts. The band irons E are fastened to the tongue C with a ³⁄₁₆ by 1½-in. stove bolt, and to corner irons F with a ³⁄₁₆-in. stove bolt.

Finishing. The Scootersled may be stained, or it may be left the natural color of the wood. The final finish should be two or three coats of good varnish.

SCOOTER SLED

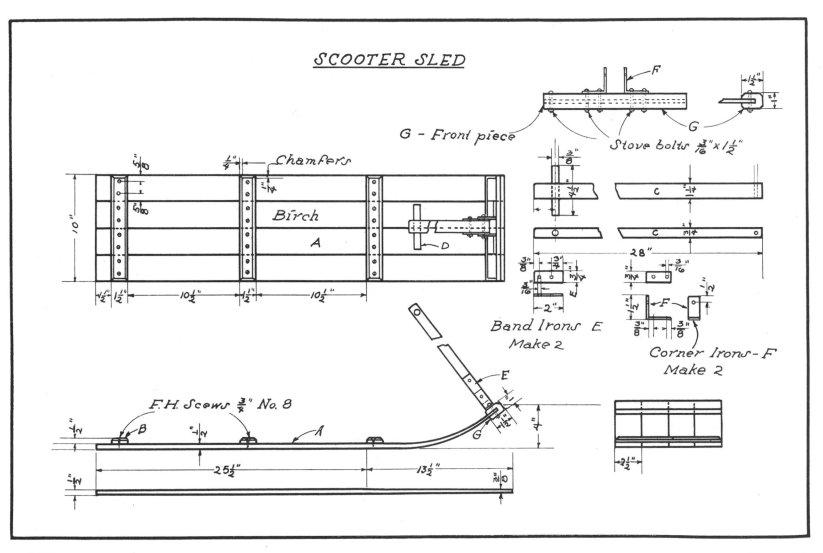

G – Front piece

Stove bolts $\frac{3}{16}'' \times 1\frac{1}{2}''$

Chamfers

Birch

A

Band Irons E
Make 2

Corner Irons – F
Make 2

F.H. Screws $\frac{3}{4}''$ No. 8

PLATE 40.   [Page 91]

TOBOGGAN

It is hardly necessary to speak of the popularity of the Toboggan with boys and girls in the northern part of this country and in Canada. Like skating, tobogganing is one of the finest and most healthful outdoor recreational activities of the winter months.

The making of a toboggan is not difficult. There are, however, a few principles of construction one should bear in mind. The selection of a straight-grained flexible wood for the runners is absolutely essential. Hickory or maple are probably the best hardwoods suitable for toboggan runners. Birch or ash may also be used with good results. Excellent results may be obtained with white, and yellow pine, but a toboggan made of pine will not be as durable as one made of the hardwood. Remember that the wood for a toboggan must be straight grained and free from knots or any other defects. A device of some kind to steam and bend the runners is essential. In Plate 42 will be found suggested devices for steaming and bending toboggan runners that have proved very successful in the writer's classes.

Bill of Material. Finished dimensions.
7 pc. ½ x 2¼ x 94   Runners (A)
7 pc. ⅝ x 2¾ x 15¾ Crosspieces (B)
2 pc. ⅝ x 1¼ x 15¾ Crosspieces (C)
1 pc. ⅞ x 1¾ x 15¾ Front Piece (D)
1 pc. Rope ½ in. diam., 15 ft. long
14 Stove Bolts 3⁄16 x 1 in.
1 doz. Large Screw Eyes.

Runners. Although 94 in. is given for the length of the runners, you may suit yourself as to the size and length of toboggan you wish to make. Plane one end of each runner A down to

¼ in. thick as shown in Plate 41. Start planing 38 in. to 40 in. from one end and gradually plane to the end until this part of the runner is wedge shape and even. This may be done with a jack plane or a smooth plane. If a power jointer is available, the planing may be done on such a machine in a very short time. The groove in the front piece D can be cut with a saw or chiseled with a ¼-in. chisel.

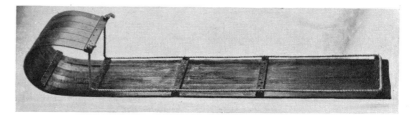

FIG. 17. TOBOGGAN.

Assembling. Fasten the five crosspieces B and the lower crosspiece C to the runners with ¾-in. No. 8 f.h. screws. Fasten the front piece D and the top piece C with 3⁄16 by 1-in. stove bolts. Bend the runners before attaching the two pieces C. The crosspieces B and the front piece D may be attached to the runners before the steaming and bending is done. The rope is held to the toboggan with large screw eyes as shown in the drawing.

Finishing. The Toboggan may be stained or it may be left the natural color of the wood. In either case the final finish should be two or more coats of varnish.

TOBOGGAN

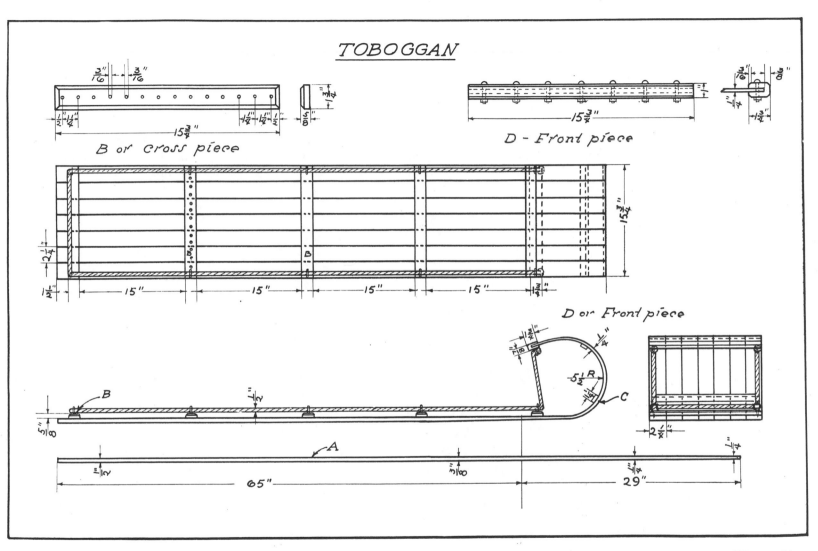

B or Cross piece

D – Front piece

D or Front piece

PLATE 41.

[Page 93]

STEAMING AND BENDING
TOBOGGAN AND SCOOTERSLED RUNNERS

The steaming and bending of toboggan runners is a very simple matter, provided that you have chosen straight-grained wood and that you have some sort of steaming barrel, box, or can, and a device to bend the runners after they are taken out of the steaming apparatus.

The steaming or boiling device illustrated in Figure 18 is nothing but a discarded oil barrel. A 1-in. iron pipe is connected to the lower part of the barrel leading to a steam pipe of the heating plant of the building. On the opposite side of the steam pipe, a faucet is fitted into the barrel to serve as an outlet for the water.

The toboggan or scootersled runners can be either steamed or boiled in this apparatus. If the wood is to be steamed, the runners should be left in the steaming barrel one hour or more. With an open barrel, like the one illustrated in Figure 18, better results can be had by using boiling water than by using steam. Allow the

FIG. 18. STEAMING OR BOILING DEVICE.

runners to remain in the water twenty to thirty minutes and bend them as quickly as possible in the bending device shown in Plate 42 and Figure 19, or some similar bending form.

FIG. 19. BENDING DEVICE.

Intense heat and long boiling tend to weaken the wood, hence, care should be taken not to steam or boil runners too long. Bend the runners slowly with an even pressure and insert the dowel rods in the holes of the bending form, one by one, until the runners are bent to the required shape. The runners of the scootersled may be bent with the same apparatus, using only the lower four dowel rods. A second method of bending scootersled runners is shown in Plate 42. Allow two days or more for drying before taking the toboggan or scootersled runners out of the bending form.

TOBOGGAN BENDING DEVICE

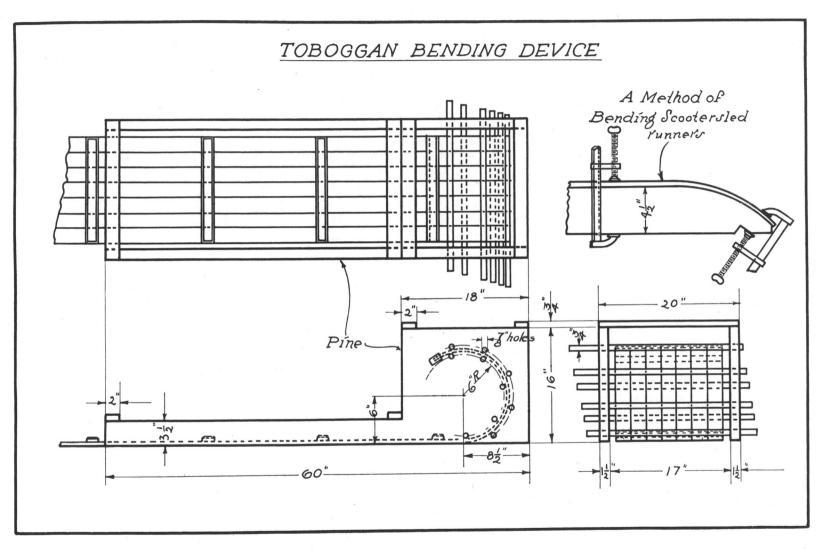

A Method of Bending Scootersled runners

Pine

PLATE 42
[Page 95]

A SCOOTER CONTEST

To encourage healthful outdoor exercise, as well as the making of boy projects, the recreation department of the park board of the city of Minneapolis promotes annually a "scooter contest."

The events of the scooter contest are arranged in two classes with two divisions in each class. The participants in Class A use manufactured scooters. The event in the first division of this class is a 75-yard race open to any boy or girl of the city under 11 years of age. The event in the second division is a 100-yard race open to any boy or girl of the city between 11 and 14 years of age.

The events of Class B are the same as those of Class A, but are only for those using homemade scooters. A gold medal as a first prize and a silver medal as a second prize for each event are donated by the recreation department.

Preliminary races are held at each of the parks to determine who shall represent each park in the final contest. In the finals, two entries in each division, a total of eight contestants, are allowed for each park, and an additional one for each six entries, or fraction thereof, above the first eight in the preliminary. At a recent contest there were 785 entries in the preliminaries and 217 in the finals.

To stimulate rivalry among the various parks and the playground instructors, the recreation department offers a special silver loving cup to the playground instructor making the best showing. The instructors are rated on the following basis: Bulletins and advertising, 1 to 30 points; local playground scooter club, 1 to 40 points; number of entries in local meet, 1 to 60 points; representatives at city club meet, 12 points each; winners at finals, 10 points for each scooter.

A PUSHMOBILE CONTEST

For several years the recreation department of the park board of the city of Minneapolis, in cooperation with the Minneapolis *Tribune* and the Maurice L. Rothschild Company, has conducted an annual "pushmobile contest."

The pushmobile contests are open to boys and girls of the city under 16 years of age. There are two events—an "ornamental" contest, and a 100-yard dash. All pushmobiles must be constructed by the contestants. There are restrictions on the amount of help the contestant may receive from adults or other boys.

Preliminary contests are conducted at each playground, the winners to represent the playground, at the final meet. Each entry consists of the pushmobile, the pilot, and the pusher.

For a recent contest, the M. L. Rothschild Company offered a pair of canvas shoes as a prize to each of the winners (pilot and pusher) in the preliminary speed contest at each playground. The prizes for the final contests donated by the Minneapolis *Tribune* were for the ornamental and construction class: two gold engraved watches, two footballs, two catcher's mitts, two balls and bats. Duplicates of the above prizes were offered for the 100-yard dash in the speed class.

There were 1,008 participants in the preliminaries and 212 in the finals of the above contest.

Another feature of the pushmobile activities at Minneapolis is the organization of a pushmobile club at each playground and the "Park Board-Minneapolis *Tribune* Pushmobile Derby Association." The *Tribune* offered a silver loving cup to the playground instructor making the best showing as follows: Bulletins and advertising, 1 to 25 points; playground pushmobile club, 1 to 10 points; number of entries in local meet, 1 to 50 points; general organization of local meet, 1 to 25 points; representatives at city club meeting, 1 to 10 points; winners at finals, 10 points per car.